ODYSSEUS

ESCAPING POSEIDON'S CURSE

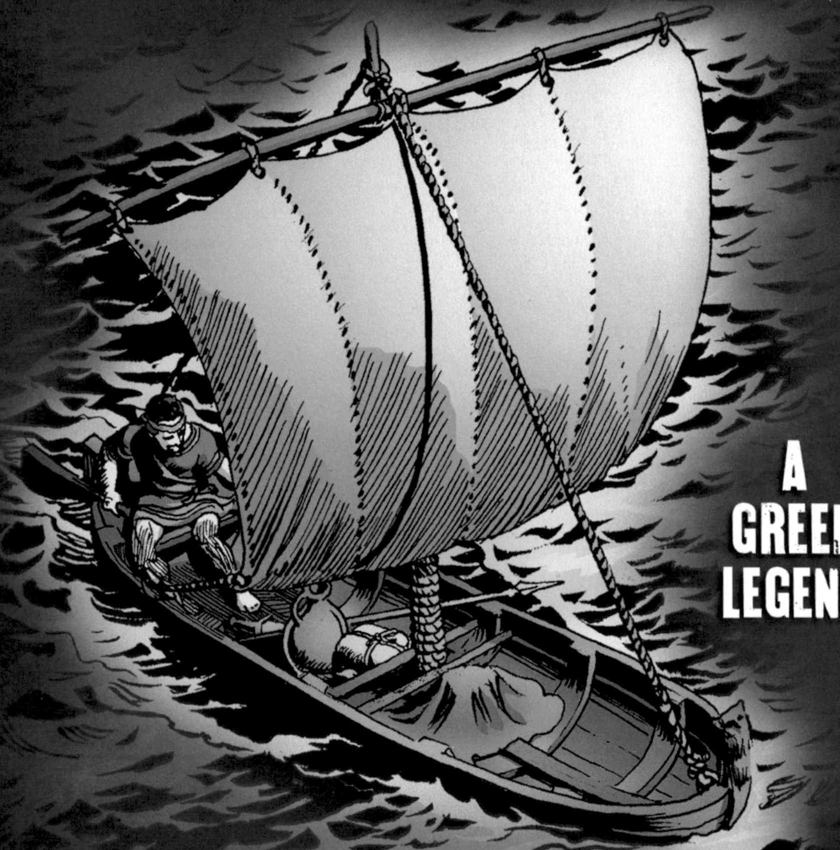

A GREEK LEGEND

GRAPHIC UNIVERSE™

STORY BY
DAN JOLLEY
PENCILS AND INKS BY
THOMAS YEATES

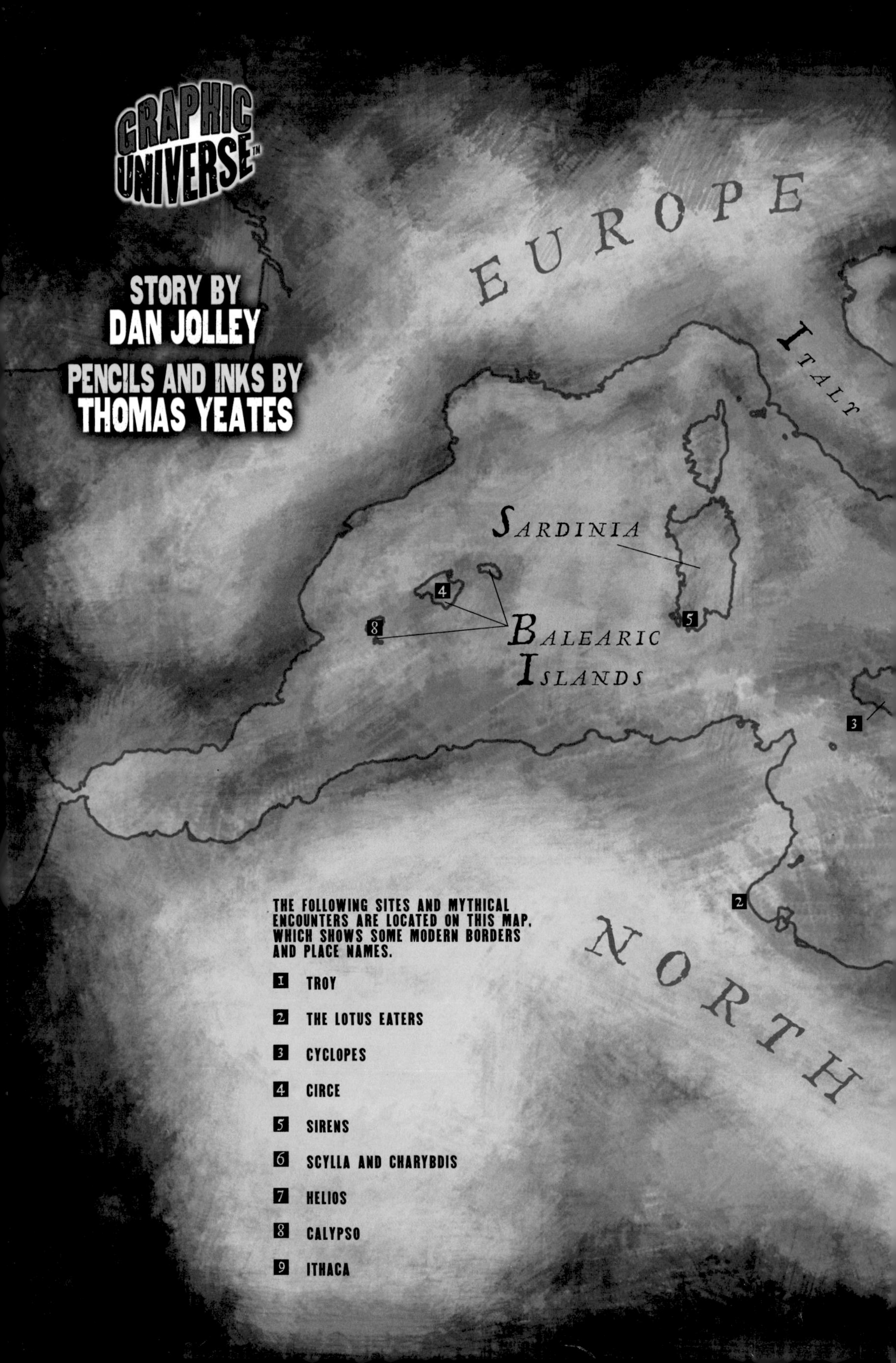

EUROPE
ITALY
SARDINIA
BALEARIC ISLANDS
NORTH
4
8
5
3
2

THE FOLLOWING SITES AND MYTHICAL ENCOUNTERS ARE LOCATED ON THIS MAP, WHICH SHOWS SOME MODERN BORDERS AND PLACE NAMES.

1 TROY

2 THE LOTUS EATERS

3 CYCLOPES

4 CIRCE

5 SIRENS

6 SCYLLA AND CHARYBDIS

7 HELIOS

8 CALYPSO

9 ITHACA

ODYSSEUS

ESCAPING POSEIDON'S CURSE

A GREEK LEGEND

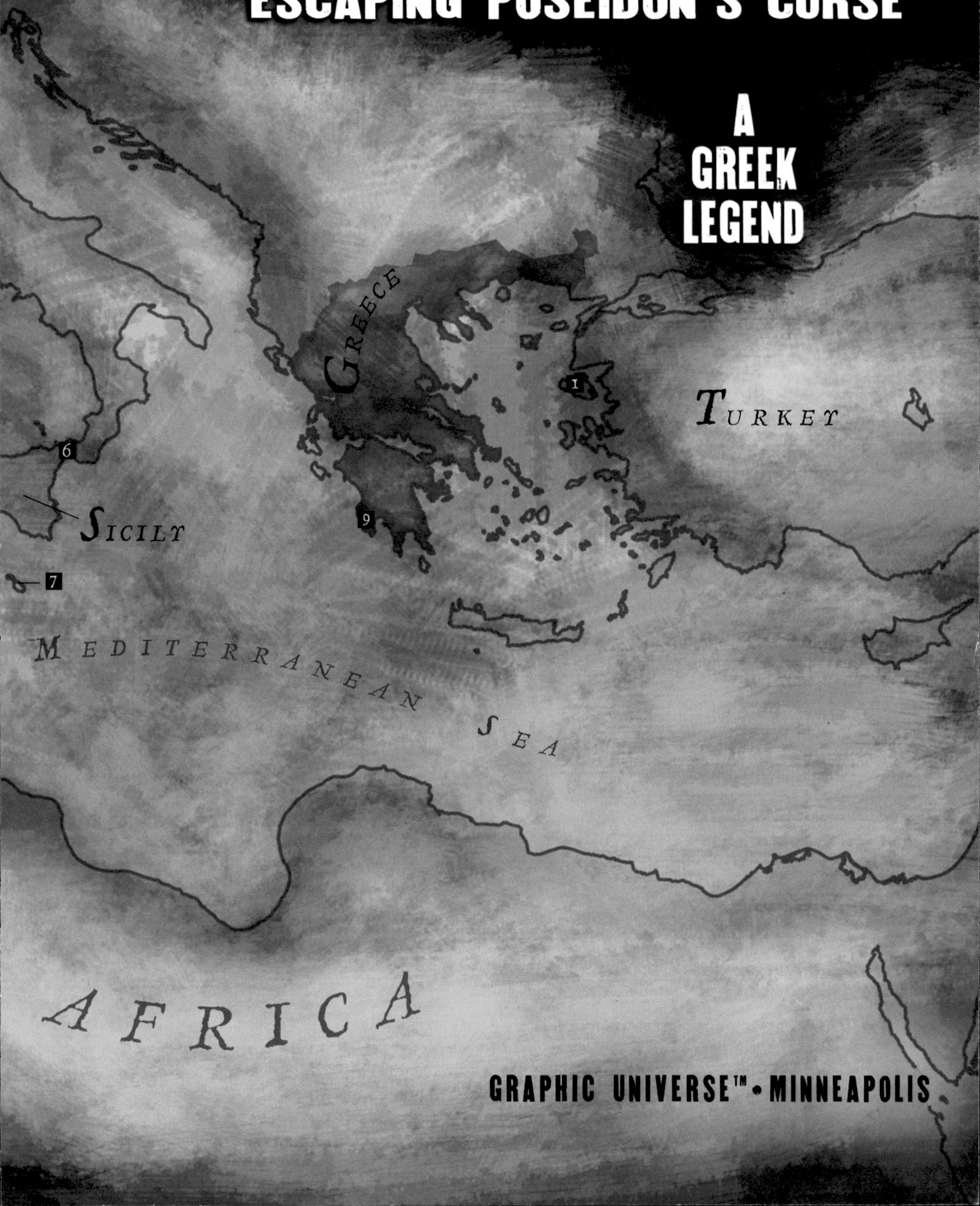

GREECE
TURKEY
SICILY
MEDITERRANEAN SEA
AFRICA
1
6
7
9

GRAPHIC UNIVERSE™ • MINNEAPOLIS

THIS BOOK IS BASED ON THE *ODYSSEY*, AN EPIC POEM BELIEVED TO HAVE BEEN WRITTEN AROUND 700 B.C. TRADITION HAS IT THAT THE STORY WAS WRITTEN BY HOMER, A BLIND GREEK POET. BUT HISTORIANS CANNOT CONFIRM THIS, AND EVEN HOMER'S EXISTENCE HAS BEEN QUESTIONED. REGARDLESS, THE EPIC STORY OF ODYSSEUS' JOURNEY HOME AFTER THE TROJAN WAR (C. 1200 B.C.) IS ONE OF THE GREATEST WORKS IN ALL OF WORLD LITERATURE.

AUTHOR DAN JOLLEY ADAPTED THE STORY TO FIT THE GRAPHIC MYTHS AND LEGENDS FORTY-PAGE FORMAT, REFERENCING SEVERAL TRANSLATIONS OF THE GREEK CLASSIC. ARTIST THOMAS YEATES USED HISTORICAL AND TRADITIONAL SOURCES FOR VISUAL DETAILS—FROM IMAGES ON ANCIENT GREEK VASES TO SCULPTURE AND OTHER ARTWORK. PROFESSOR DAVID MULROY OF THE UNIVERSITY OF WISCONSIN-MILWAUKEE ENSURED HISTORICAL AND VISUAL ACCURACY.

STORY BY DAN JOLLEY

PENCILS AND INKS BY THOMAS YEATES
WITH SAM GLANZMAN AND KEN HOOPER

COLORING AND LETTERING BY
HI-FI COLOUR DESIGN

CONSULTANT: DAVID MULROY, PH.D.,
UNIVERSITY OF WISCONSIN—MILWAUKEE

Graphic Universe™
A division of Lerner Publishing Group, Inc.
241 First Avenue North
Minneapolis, MN 55401 U.S.A.

Website: www.lernerbooks.com

Library of Congress Cataloging-in-Publication Data

Jolley, Dan.
    Odysseus : escaping Poseidon's curse : a Greek legend / story by Dan Jolley ; pencils and inks by Thomas Yeates.
        p.   cm. — (Graphic myths and legends)
    Includes index.
    ISBN-13: 978-0-8225-6208-5 (lib. bdg. : alk. paper)
    1. Odysseus (Greek mythology)—Juvenile literature. 2. Poseidon (Greek deity)—Juvenile literature. I. Yeates, Thomas. II. Title.
    BL820.O3J65   2008
    741.5'973—dc22   2007001827

Manufactured in the United States of America
1 2 3 4 5 6 - JR - 13 12 10 09 08

TABLE OF CONTENTS

THE JOURNEY BEGINS...6

THE FURY OF THE CYCLOPS...12

THE MAGIC OF THE ISLAND WITCH...21

AN ORDEAL OF MONSTERS...29

A TEMPTATION TOO GREAT...35

CALYPSO'S EMBRACE...39

GLOSSARY AND PRONUNCIATION GUIDE...46

FURTHER READING, WEBSITES, AND MOVIES...47

CREATING *ODYSSEUS: ESCAPING POSEIDON'S CURSE*...47

INDEX...48

ABOUT THE AUTHOR AND THE ARTIST...48

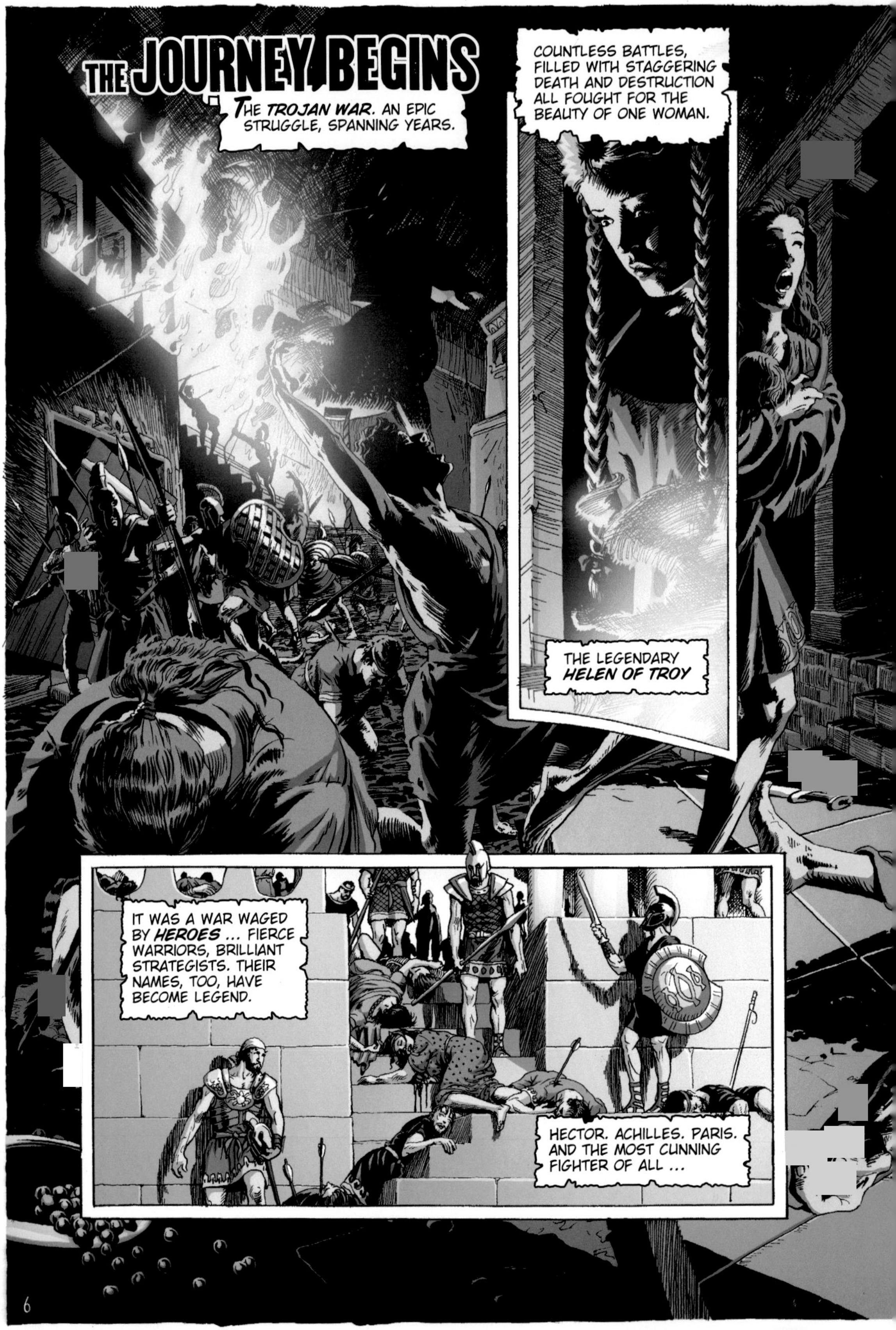
THE JOURNEY BEGINS
THE TROJAN WAR. AN EPIC STRUGGLE, SPANNING YEARS.
COUNTLESS BATTLES, FILLED WITH STAGGERING DEATH AND DESTRUCTION ALL FOUGHT FOR THE BEAUTY OF ONE WOMAN.
THE LEGENDARY HELEN OF TROY
IT WAS A WAR WAGED BY HEROES ... FIERCE WARRIORS, BRILLIANT STRATEGISTS. THEIR NAMES, TOO, HAVE BECOME LEGEND.
HECTOR. ACHILLES. PARIS. AND THE MOST CUNNING FIGHTER OF ALL ...

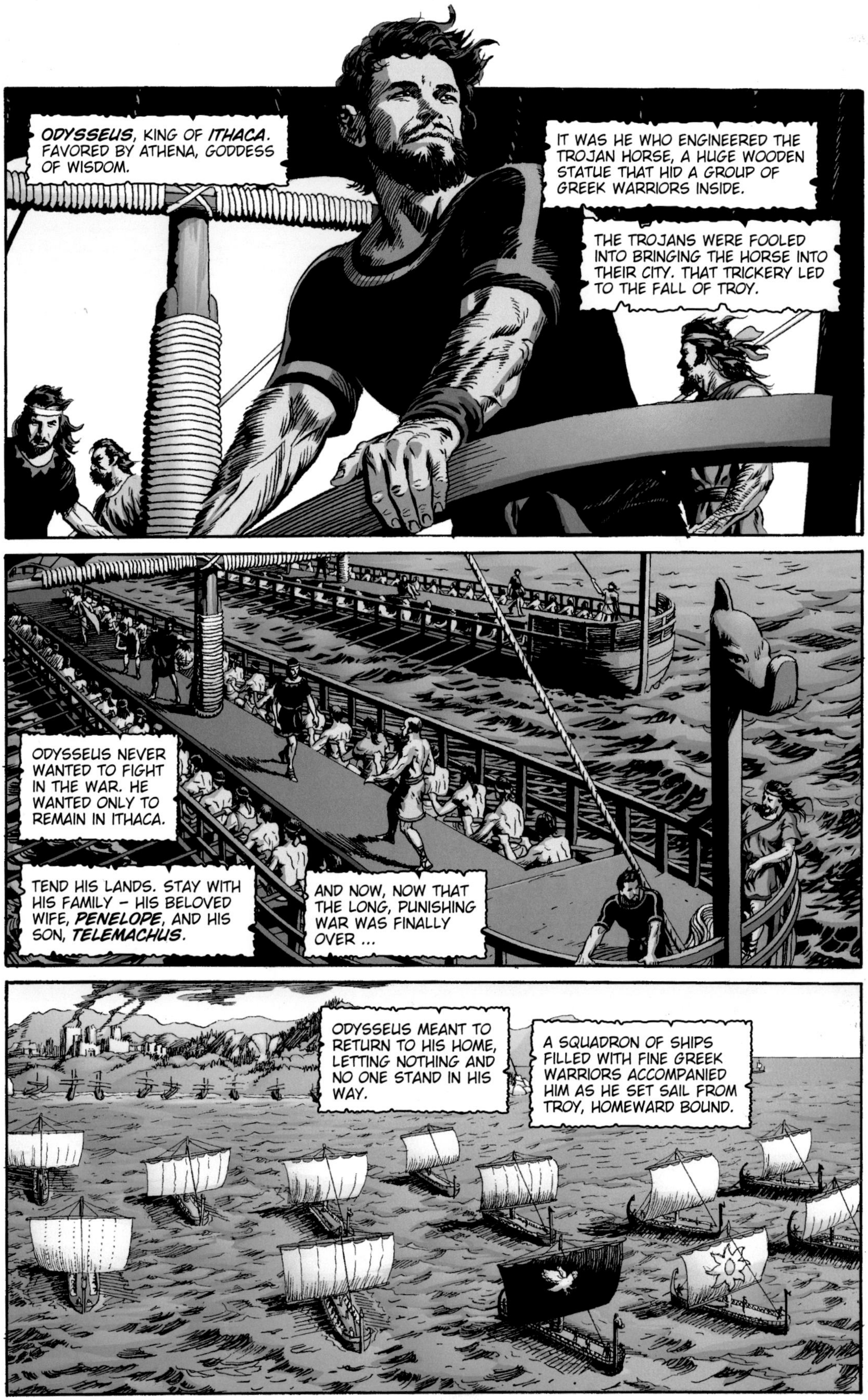
ODYSSEUS, KING OF ***ITHACA***. FAVORED BY ATHENA, GODDESS OF WISDOM.
IT WAS HE WHO ENGINEERED THE TROJAN HORSE, A HUGE WOODEN STATUE THAT HID A GROUP OF GREEK WARRIORS INSIDE.
THE TROJANS WERE FOOLED INTO BRINGING THE HORSE INTO THEIR CITY. THAT TRICKERY LED TO THE FALL OF TROY.
ODYSSEUS NEVER WANTED TO FIGHT IN THE WAR. HE WANTED ONLY TO REMAIN IN ITHACA.
TEND HIS LANDS. STAY WITH HIS FAMILY – HIS BELOVED WIFE, ***PENELOPE***, AND HIS SON, ***TELEMACHUS***.
AND NOW, NOW THAT THE LONG, PUNISHING WAR WAS FINALLY OVER ...
ODYSSEUS MEANT TO RETURN TO HIS HOME, LETTING NOTHING AND NO ONE STAND IN HIS WAY.
A SQUADRON OF SHIPS FILLED WITH FINE GREEK WARRIORS ACCOMPANIED HIM AS HE SET SAIL FROM TROY, HOMEWARD BOUND.

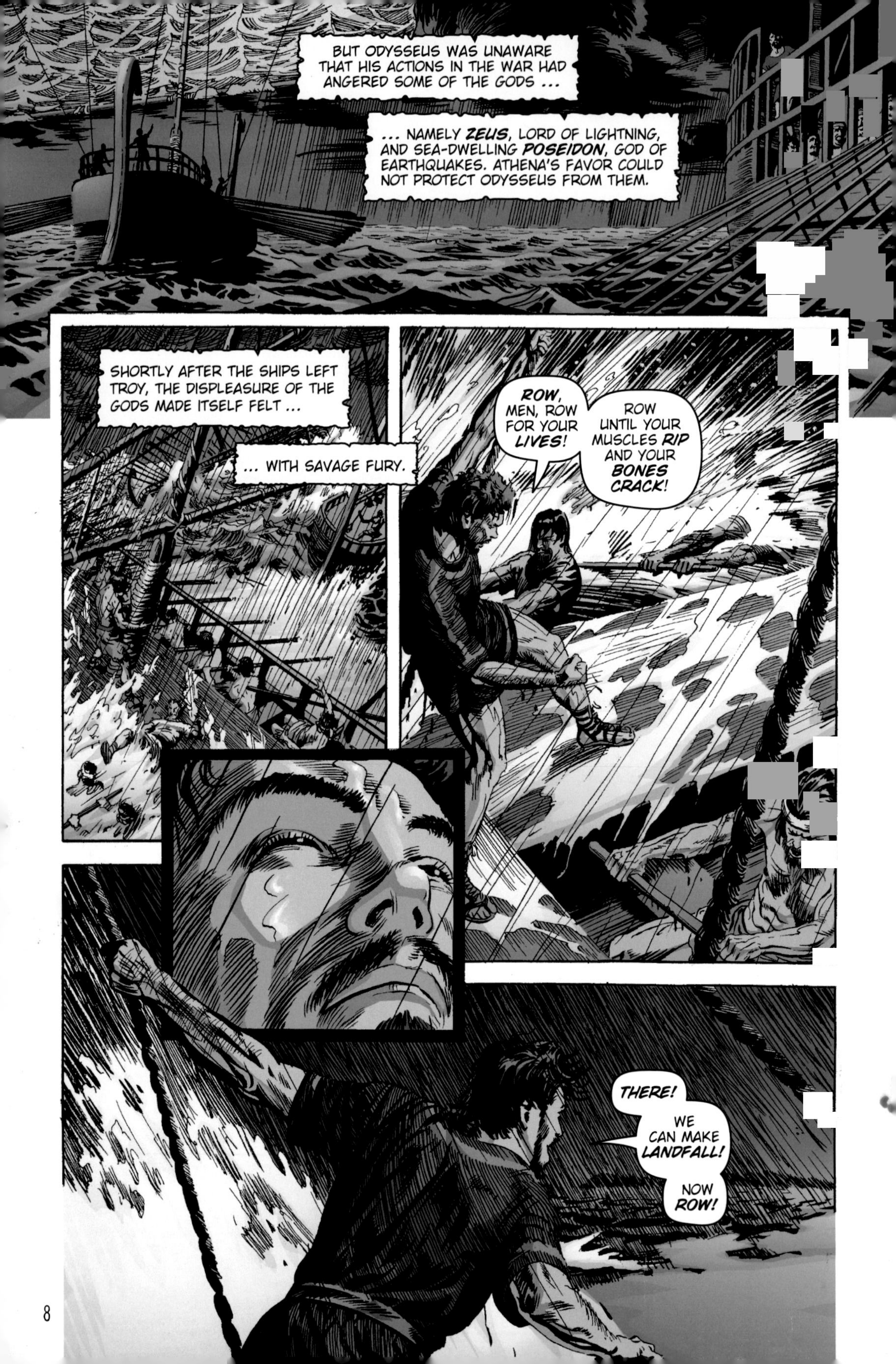
BUT ODYSSEUS WAS UNAWARE THAT HIS ACTIONS IN THE WAR HAD ANGERED SOME OF THE GODS ...
... NAMELY ZEUS, LORD OF LIGHTNING, AND SEA-DWELLING POSEIDON, GOD OF EARTHQUAKES. ATHENA'S FAVOR COULD NOT PROTECT ODYSSEUS FROM THEM.
SHORTLY AFTER THE SHIPS LEFT TROY, THE DISPLEASURE OF THE GODS MADE ITSELF FELT ...
... WITH SAVAGE FURY.
ROW, MEN, ROW FOR YOUR LIVES!
ROW UNTIL YOUR MUSCLES RIP AND YOUR BONES CRACK!
THERE!
WE CAN MAKE LANDFALL!
NOW ROW!

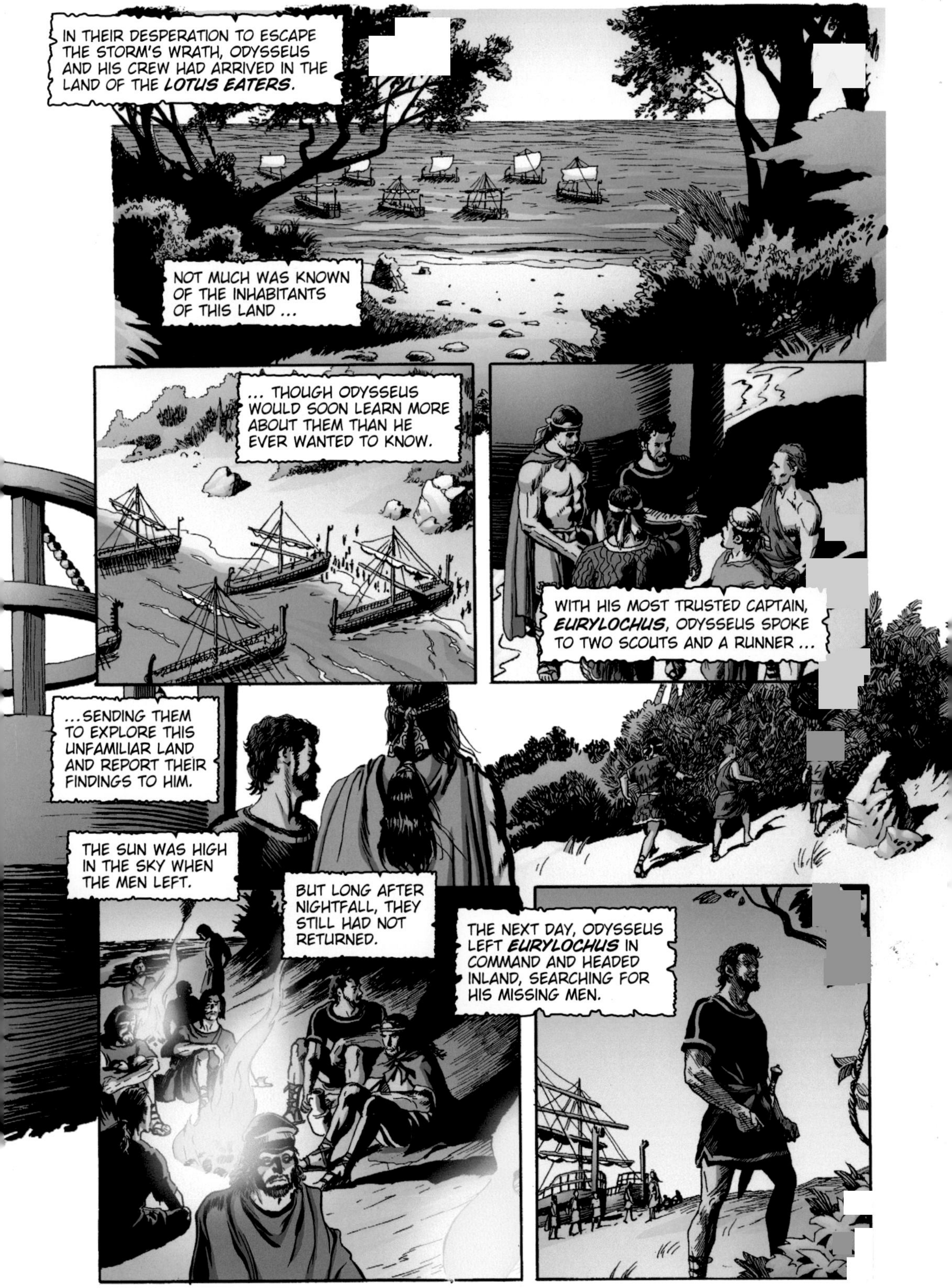

IN THEIR DESPERATION TO ESCAPE THE STORM'S WRATH, ODYSSEUS AND HIS CREW HAD ARRIVED IN THE LAND OF THE LOTUS EATERS.
NOT MUCH WAS KNOWN OF THE INHABITANTS OF THIS LAND ...
... THOUGH ODYSSEUS WOULD SOON LEARN MORE ABOUT THEM THAN HE EVER WANTED TO KNOW.
WITH HIS MOST TRUSTED CAPTAIN, EURYLOCHUS, ODYSSEUS SPOKE TO TWO SCOUTS AND A RUNNER ...
...SENDING THEM TO EXPLORE THIS UNFAMILIAR LAND AND REPORT THEIR FINDINGS TO HIM.
THE SUN WAS HIGH IN THE SKY WHEN THE MEN LEFT.
BUT LONG AFTER NIGHTFALL, THEY STILL HAD NOT RETURNED.
THE NEXT DAY, ODYSSEUS LEFT EURYLOCHUS IN COMMAND AND HEADED INLAND, SEARCHING FOR HIS MISSING MEN.

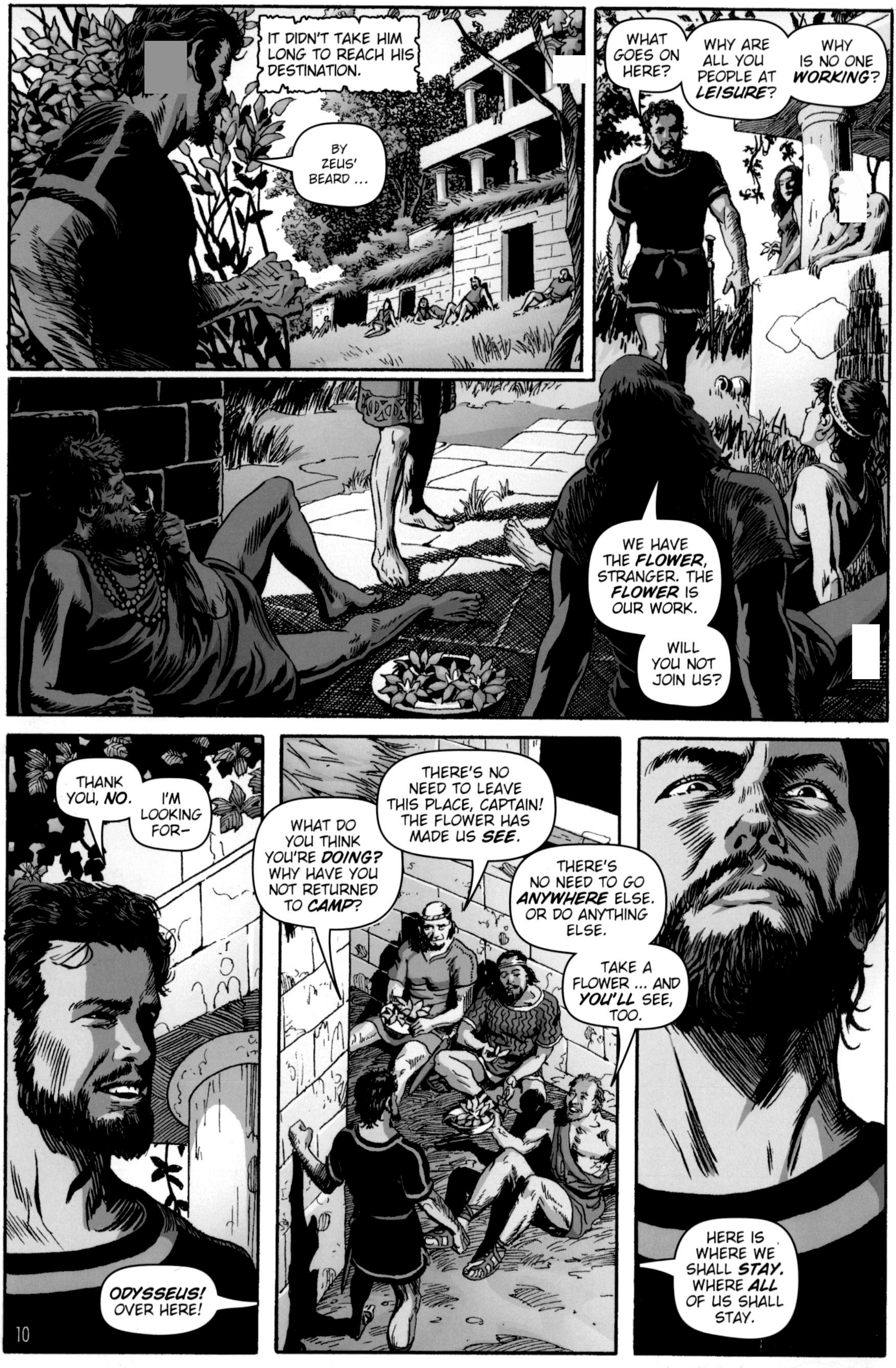
IT DIDN'T TAKE HIM LONG TO REACH HIS DESTINATION.
BY ZEUS' BEARD ...
WHAT GOES ON HERE?
WHY ARE ALL YOU PEOPLE AT LEISURE?
WHY IS NO ONE WORKING?
WE HAVE THE FLOWER, STRANGER. THE FLOWER IS OUR WORK.
WILL YOU NOT JOIN US?
THANK YOU, NO.
I'M LOOKING FOR-
ODYSSEUS! OVER HERE!
WHAT DO YOU THINK YOU'RE DOING? WHY HAVE YOU NOT RETURNED TO CAMP?
THERE'S NO NEED TO LEAVE THIS PLACE, CAPTAIN! THE FLOWER HAS MADE US SEE.
THERE'S NO NEED TO GO ANYWHERE ELSE. OR DO ANYTHING ELSE.
TAKE A FLOWER ... AND YOU'LL SEE, TOO.
HERE IS WHERE WE SHALL STAY. WHERE ALL OF US SHALL STAY.

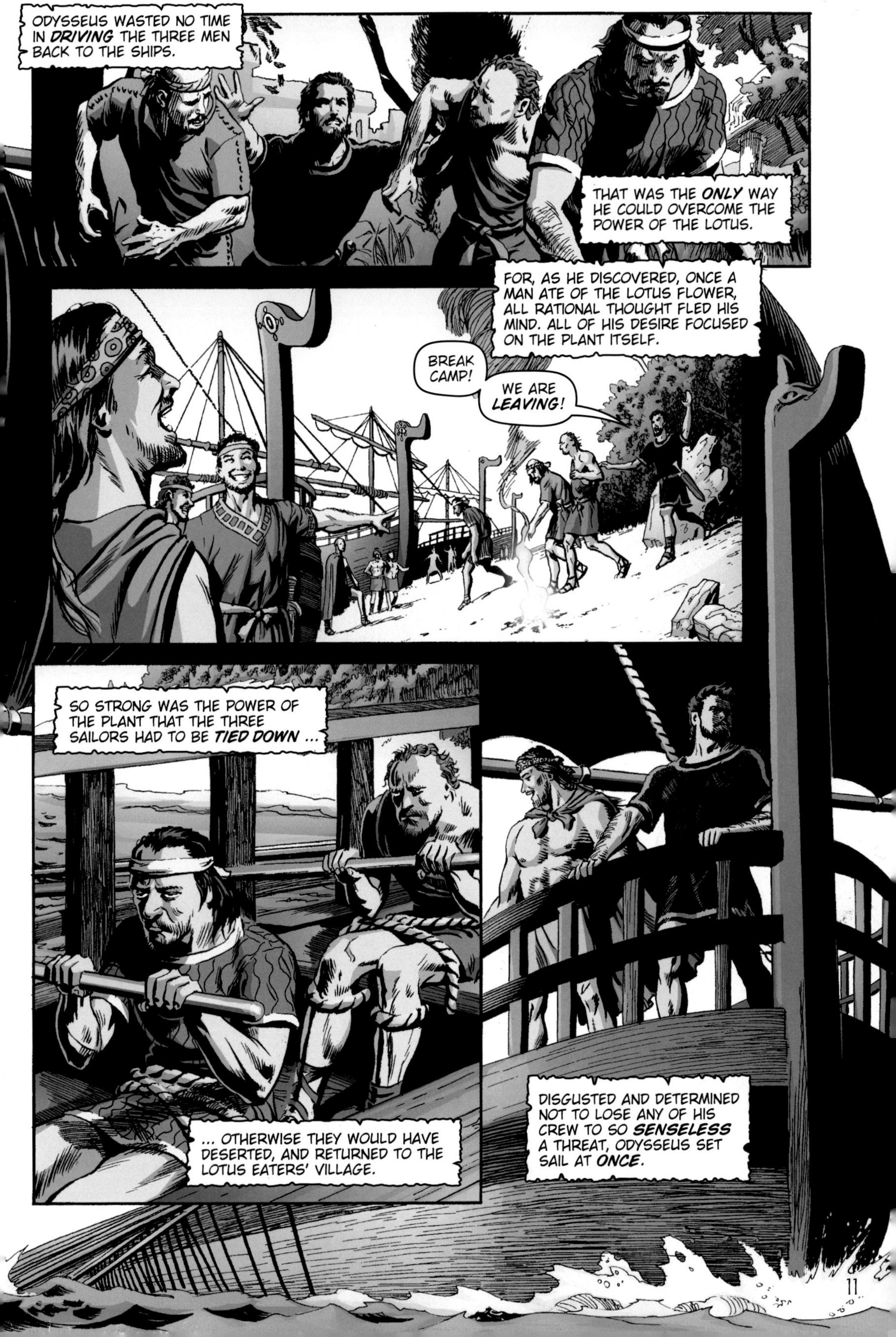

ODYSSEUS WASTED NO TIME IN DRIVING THE THREE MEN BACK TO THE SHIPS.
THAT WAS THE ONLY WAY HE COULD OVERCOME THE POWER OF THE LOTUS.
FOR, AS HE DISCOVERED, ONCE A MAN ATE OF THE LOTUS FLOWER, ALL RATIONAL THOUGHT FLED HIS MIND. ALL OF HIS DESIRE FOCUSED ON THE PLANT ITSELF.
BREAK CAMP!
WE ARE LEAVING!
SO STRONG WAS THE POWER OF THE PLANT THAT THE THREE SAILORS HAD TO BE TIED DOWN ...
... OTHERWISE THEY WOULD HAVE DESERTED, AND RETURNED TO THE LOTUS EATERS' VILLAGE.
DISGUSTED AND DETERMINED NOT TO LOSE ANY OF HIS CREW TO SO SENSELESS A THREAT, ODYSSEUS SET SAIL AT ONCE.

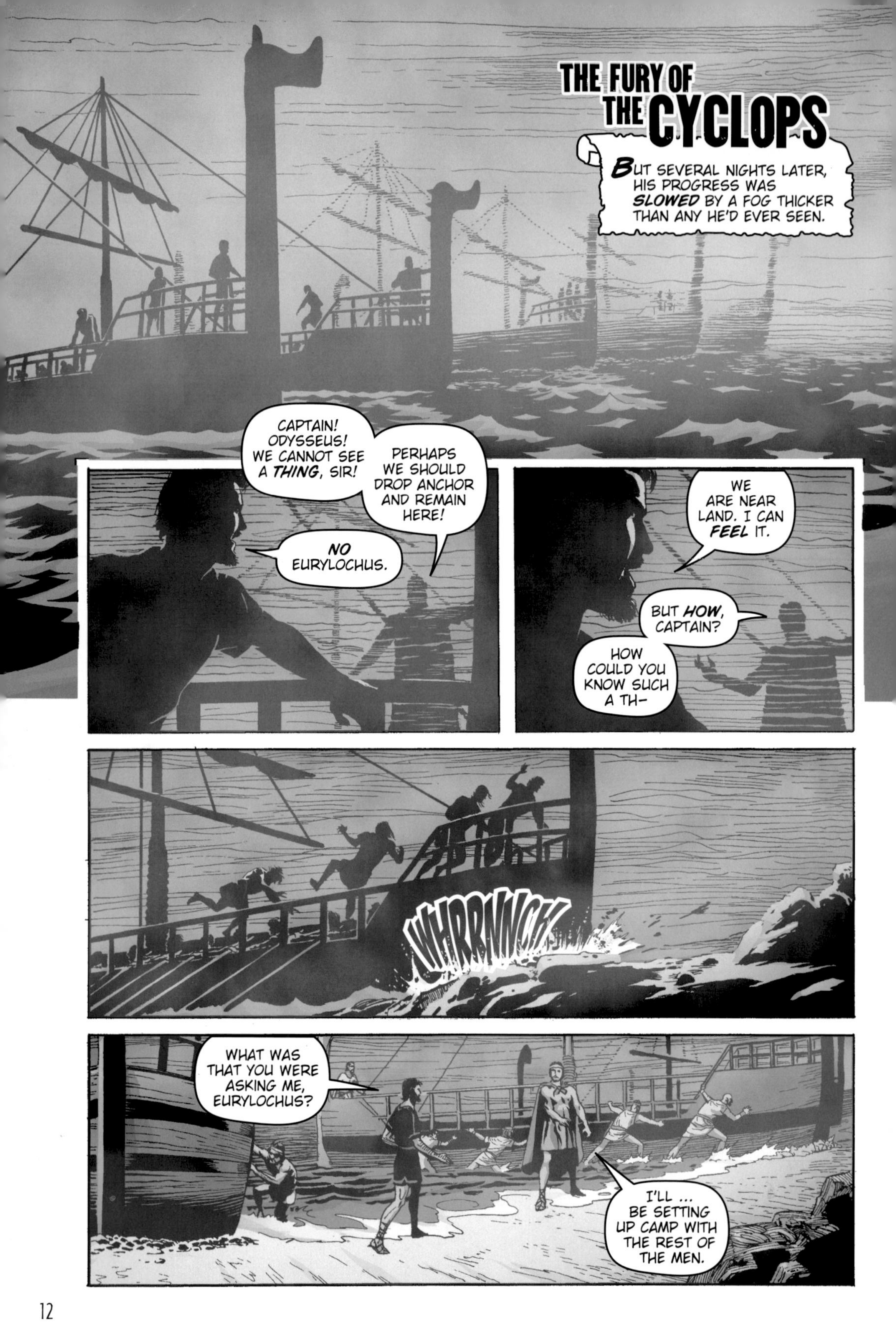

THE FURY OF THE CYCLOPS
BUT SEVERAL NIGHTS LATER, HIS PROGRESS WAS SLOWED BY A FOG THICKER THAN ANY HE'D EVER SEEN.
CAPTAIN! ODYSSEUS! WE CANNOT SEE A THING, SIR!
PERHAPS WE SHOULD DROP ANCHOR AND REMAIN HERE!
NO EURYLOCHUS.
WE ARE NEAR LAND. I CAN FEEL IT.
BUT HOW, CAPTAIN?
HOW COULD YOU KNOW SUCH A TH–
WHRRNNCH!
WHAT WAS THAT YOU WERE ASKING ME, EURYLOCHUS?
I'LL ... BE SETTING UP CAMP WITH THE REST OF THE MEN.

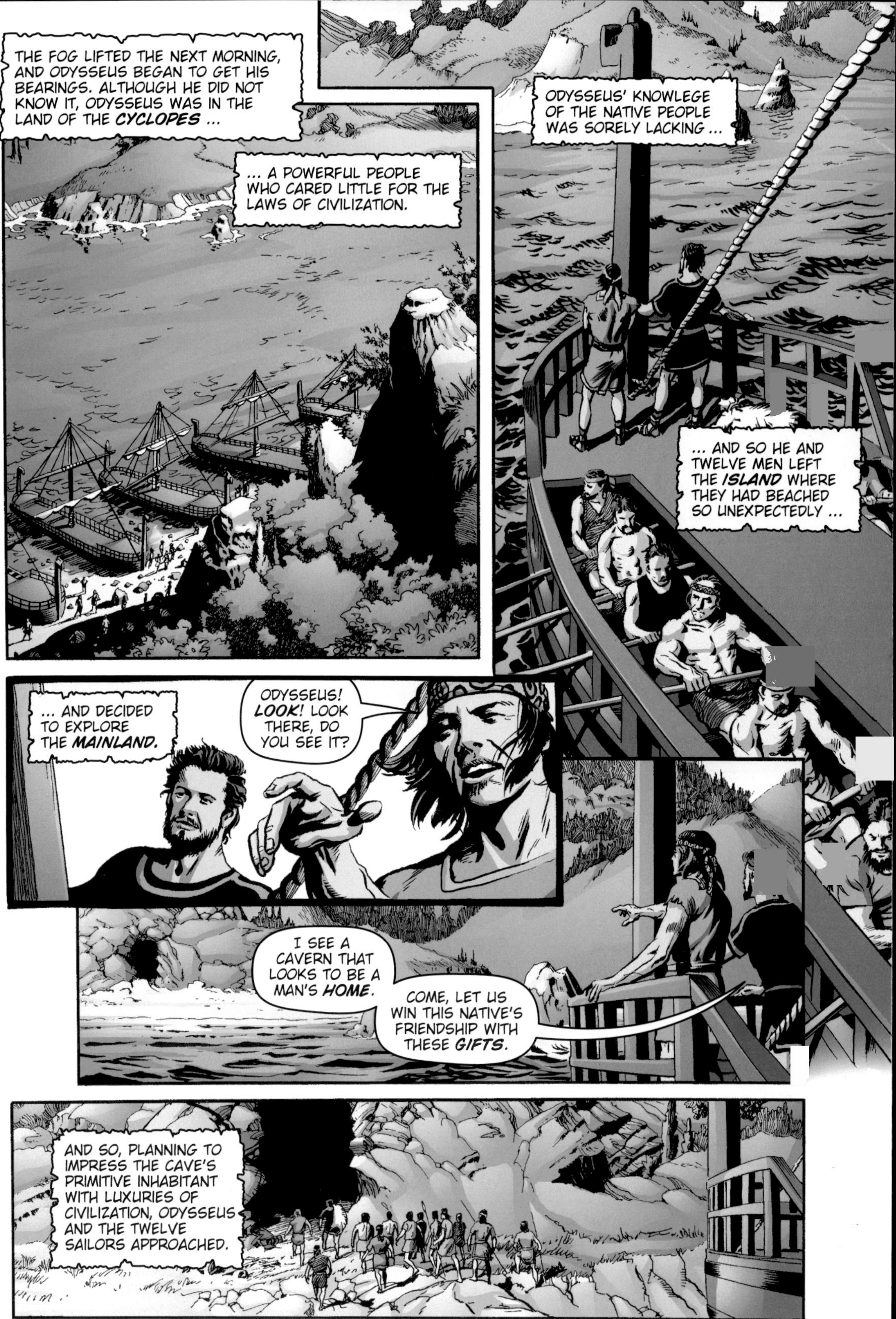
THE FOG LIFTED THE NEXT MORNING, AND ODYSSEUS BEGAN TO GET HIS BEARINGS. ALTHOUGH HE DID NOT KNOW IT, ODYSSEUS WAS IN THE LAND OF THE CYCLOPES ...
... A POWERFUL PEOPLE WHO CARED LITTLE FOR THE LAWS OF CIVILIZATION.
ODYSSEUS' KNOWLEGE OF THE NATIVE PEOPLE WAS SORELY LACKING ...
... AND SO HE AND TWELVE MEN LEFT THE ISLAND WHERE THEY HAD BEACHED SO UNEXPECTEDLY ...
... AND DECIDED TO EXPLORE THE MAINLAND.
ODYSSEUS! LOOK! LOOK THERE, DO YOU SEE IT?
I SEE A CAVERN THAT LOOKS TO BE A MAN'S HOME.
COME, LET US WIN THIS NATIVE'S FRIENDSHIP WITH THESE GIFTS.
AND SO, PLANNING TO IMPRESS THE CAVE'S PRIMITIVE INHABITANT WITH LUXURIES OF CIVILIZATION, ODYSSEUS AND THE TWELVE SAILORS APPROACHED.

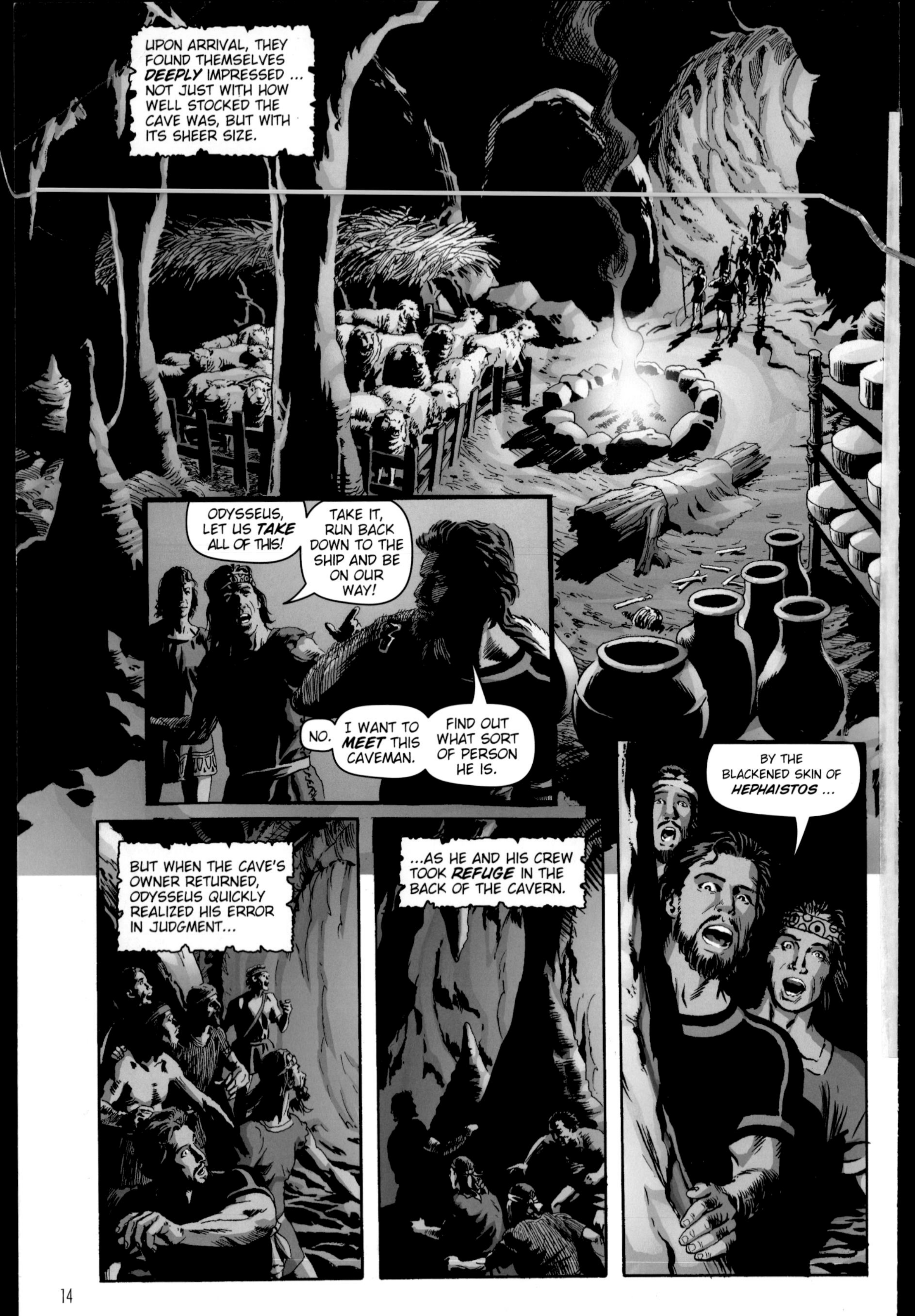
UPON ARRIVAL, THEY FOUND THEMSELVES DEEPLY IMPRESSED ... NOT JUST WITH HOW WELL STOCKED THE CAVE WAS, BUT WITH ITS SHEER SIZE.
ODYSSEUS, LET US TAKE ALL OF THIS!
TAKE IT, RUN BACK DOWN TO THE SHIP AND BE ON OUR WAY!
NO.
I WANT TO MEET THIS CAVEMAN.
FIND OUT WHAT SORT OF PERSON HE IS.
BUT WHEN THE CAVE'S OWNER RETURNED, ODYSSEUS QUICKLY REALIZED HIS ERROR IN JUDGMENT...
...AS HE AND HIS CREW TOOK REFUGE IN THE BACK OF THE CAVERN.
BY THE BLACKENED SKIN OF HEPHAISTOS ...

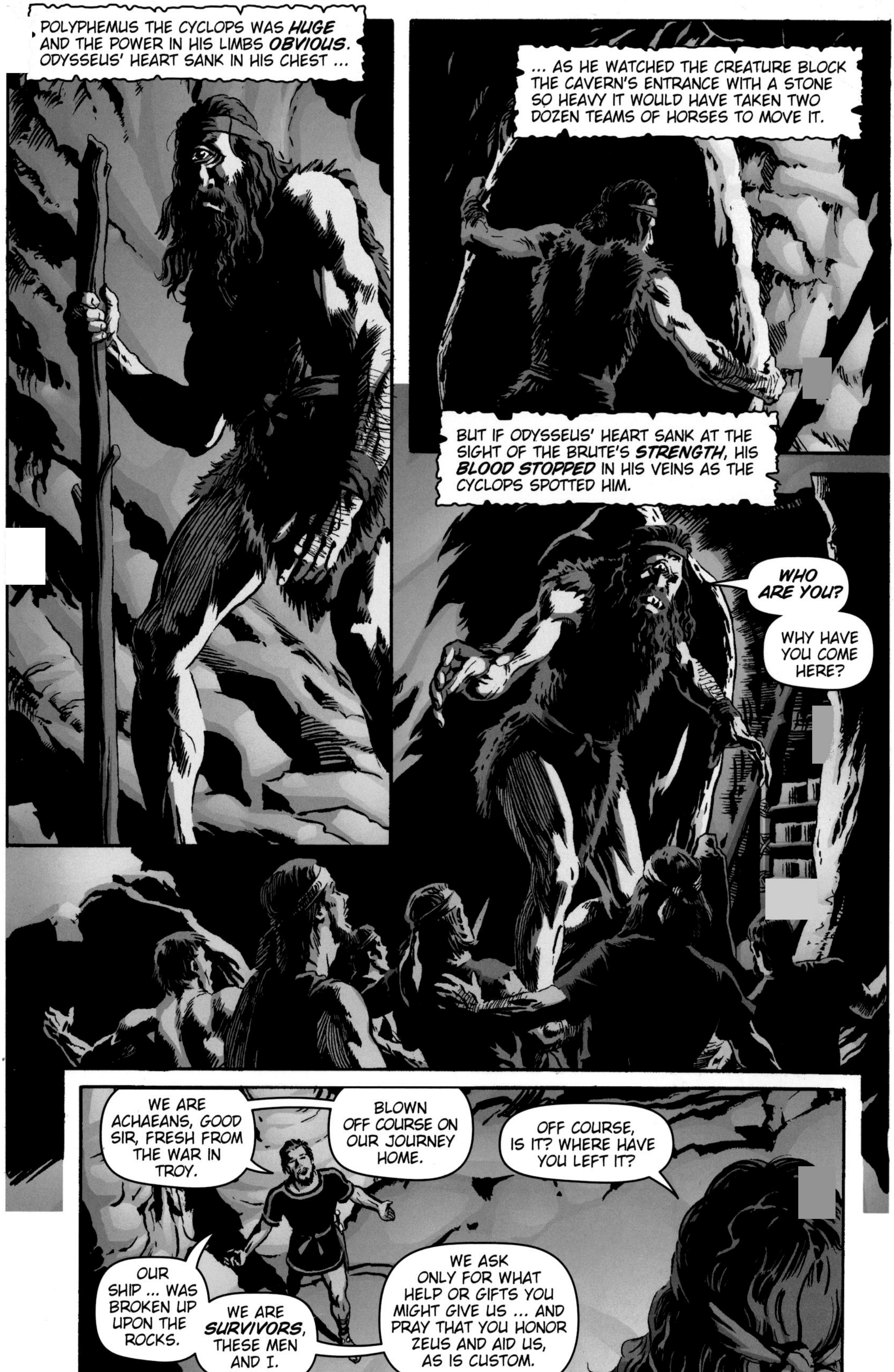
POLYPHEMUS THE CYCLOPS WAS **HUGE** AND THE POWER IN HIS LIMBS **OBVIOUS.** ODYSSEUS' HEART SANK IN HIS CHEST ...
... AS HE WATCHED THE CREATURE BLOCK THE CAVERN'S ENTRANCE WITH A STONE SO HEAVY IT WOULD HAVE TAKEN TWO DOZEN TEAMS OF HORSES TO MOVE IT.
BUT IF ODYSSEUS' HEART SANK AT THE SIGHT OF THE BRUTE'S **STRENGTH**, HIS **BLOOD STOPPED** IN HIS VEINS AS THE CYCLOPS SPOTTED HIM.
WHO ARE YOU?
WHY HAVE YOU COME HERE?
WE ARE ACHAEANS, GOOD SIR, FRESH FROM THE WAR IN TROY.
BLOWN OFF COURSE ON OUR JOURNEY HOME.
OFF COURSE, IS IT? WHERE HAVE YOU LEFT IT?
OUR SHIP ... WAS BROKEN UP UPON THE ROCKS.
WE ARE **SURVIVORS**, THESE MEN AND I.
WE ASK ONLY FOR WHAT HELP OR GIFTS YOU MIGHT GIVE US ... AND PRAY THAT YOU HONOR ZEUS AND AID US, AS IS CUSTOM.

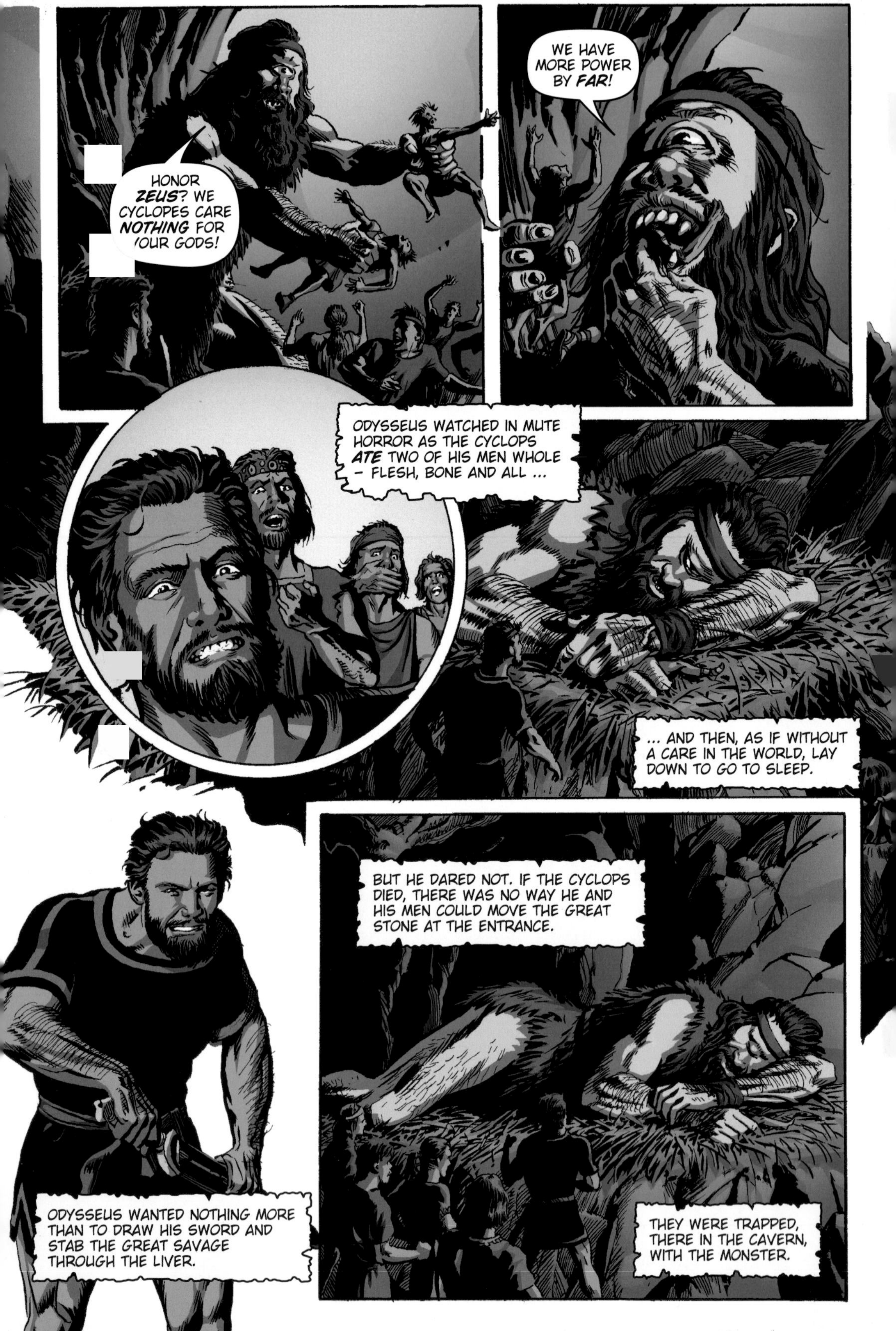
HONOR ZEUS? WE CYCLOPES CARE NOTHING FOR YOUR GODS!
WE HAVE MORE POWER BY FAR!
ODYSSEUS WATCHED IN MUTE HORROR AS THE CYCLOPS ATE TWO OF HIS MEN WHOLE – FLESH, BONE AND ALL ...
... AND THEN, AS IF WITHOUT A CARE IN THE WORLD, LAY DOWN TO GO TO SLEEP.
ODYSSEUS WANTED NOTHING MORE THAN TO DRAW HIS SWORD AND STAB THE GREAT SAVAGE THROUGH THE LIVER.
BUT HE DARED NOT. IF THE CYCLOPS DIED, THERE WAS NO WAY HE AND HIS MEN COULD MOVE THE GREAT STONE AT THE ENTRANCE.
THEY WERE TRAPPED, THERE IN THE CAVERN, WITH THE MONSTER.

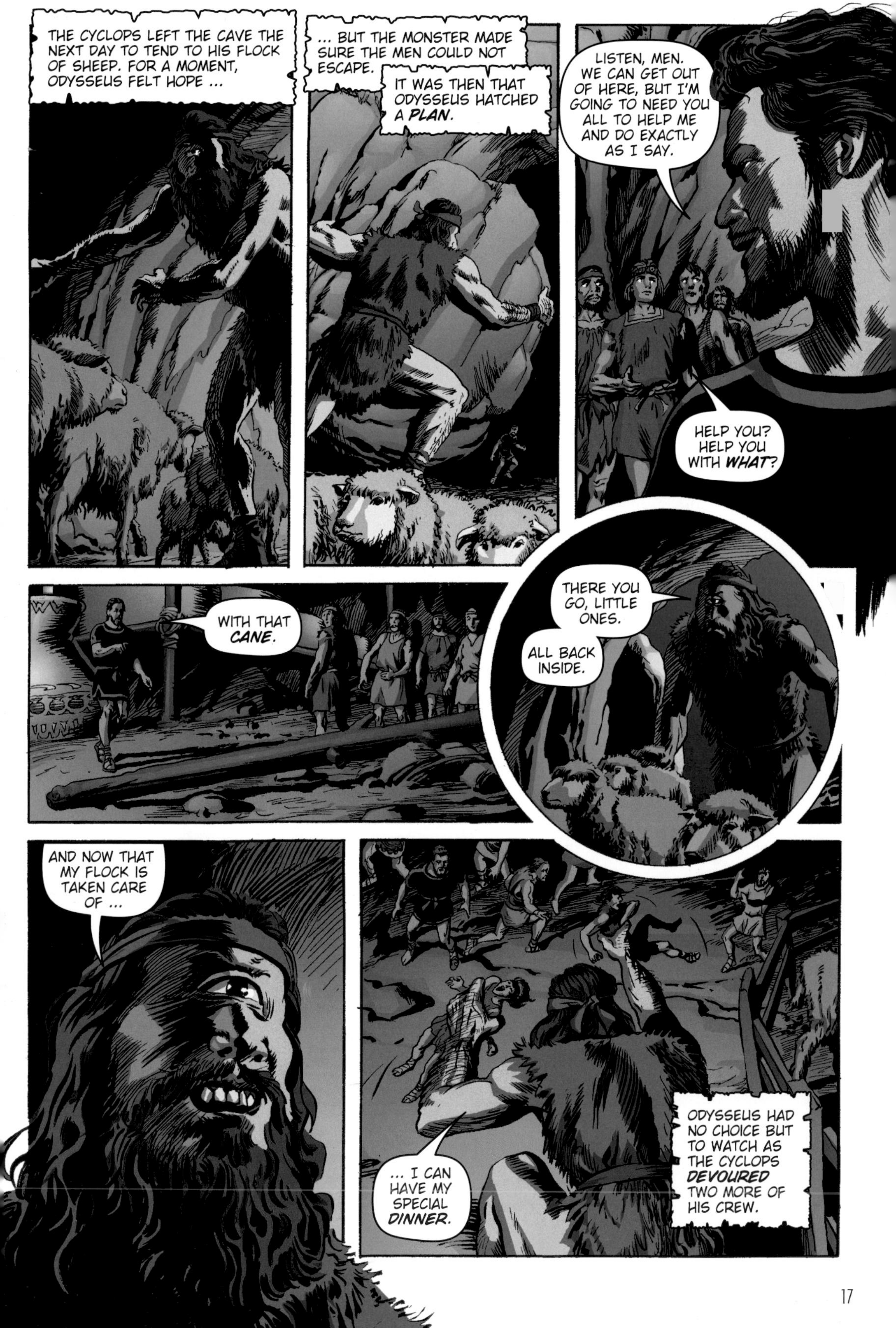
THE CYCLOPS LEFT THE CAVE THE NEXT DAY TO TEND TO HIS FLOCK OF SHEEP. FOR A MOMENT, ODYSSEUS FELT HOPE ...
... BUT THE MONSTER MADE SURE THE MEN COULD NOT ESCAPE.
IT WAS THEN THAT ODYSSEUS HATCHED A *PLAN*.
LISTEN, MEN. WE CAN GET OUT OF HERE, BUT I'M GOING TO NEED YOU ALL TO HELP ME AND DO EXACTLY AS I SAY.
HELP YOU? HELP YOU WITH *WHAT*?
WITH THAT *CANE*.
THERE YOU GO, LITTLE ONES.
ALL BACK INSIDE.
AND NOW THAT MY FLOCK IS TAKEN CARE OF ...
... I CAN HAVE MY SPECIAL *DINNER*.
ODYSSEUS HAD NO CHOICE BUT TO WATCH AS THE CYCLOPS *DEVOURED* TWO MORE OF HIS CREW.

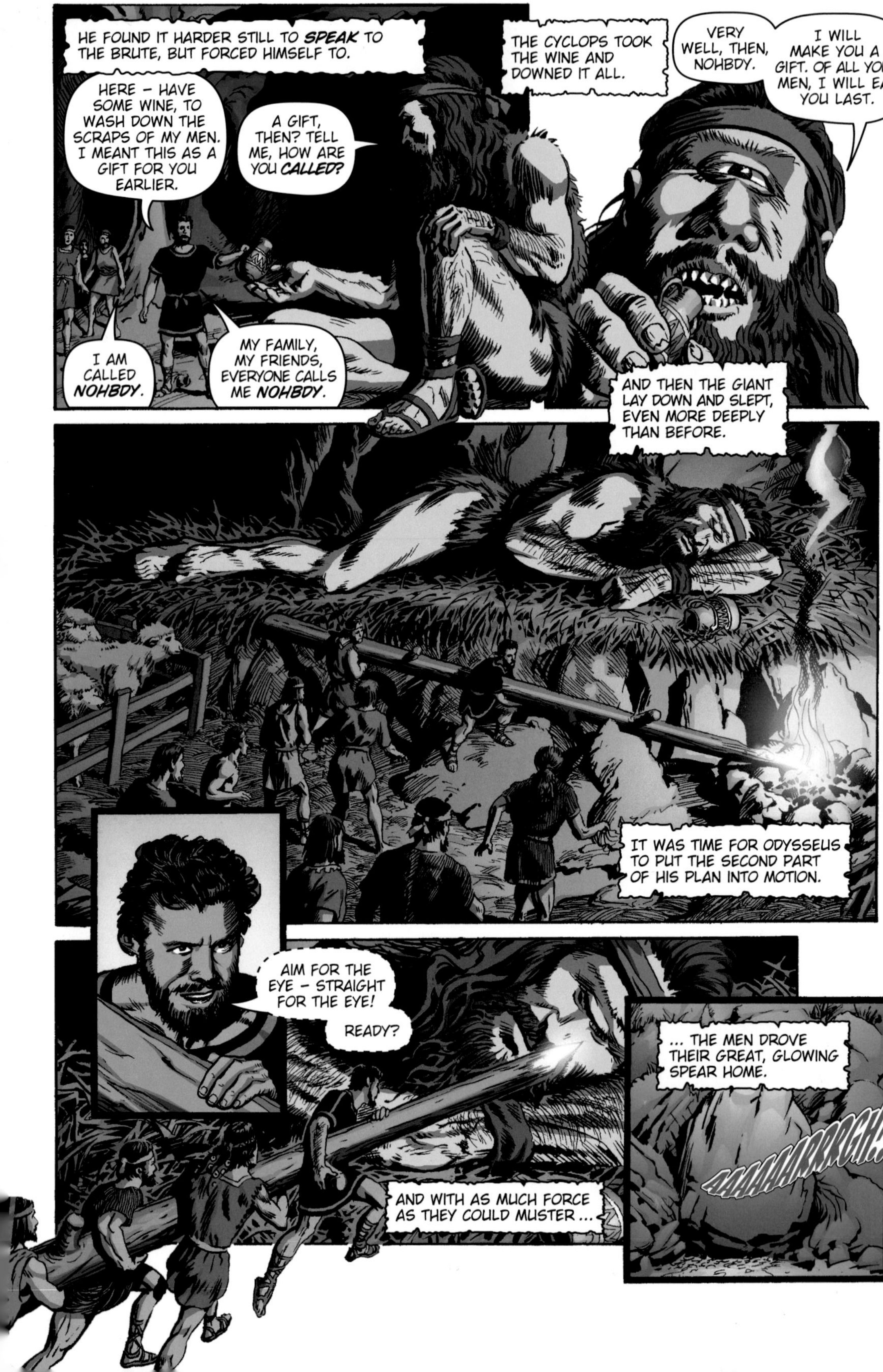
HE FOUND IT HARDER STILL TO SPEAK TO THE BRUTE, BUT FORCED HIMSELF TO.
HERE – HAVE SOME WINE, TO WASH DOWN THE SCRAPS OF MY MEN. I MEANT THIS AS A GIFT FOR YOU EARLIER.
A GIFT, THEN? TELL ME, HOW ARE YOU CALLED?
I AM CALLED NOHBDY.
MY FAMILY, MY FRIENDS, EVERYONE CALLS ME NOHBDY.
THE CYCLOPS TOOK THE WINE AND DOWNED IT ALL.
VERY WELL, THEN, NOHBDY.
I WILL MAKE YOU A GIFT. OF ALL YOUR MEN, I WILL EAT YOU LAST.
AND THEN THE GIANT LAY DOWN AND SLEPT, EVEN MORE DEEPLY THAN BEFORE.
IT WAS TIME FOR ODYSSEUS TO PUT THE SECOND PART OF HIS PLAN INTO MOTION.
AIM FOR THE EYE – STRAIGHT FOR THE EYE!
READY?
AND WITH AS MUCH FORCE AS THEY COULD MUSTER ...
... THE MEN DROVE THEIR GREAT, GLOWING SPEAR HOME.
AAAAAARRRGH!!

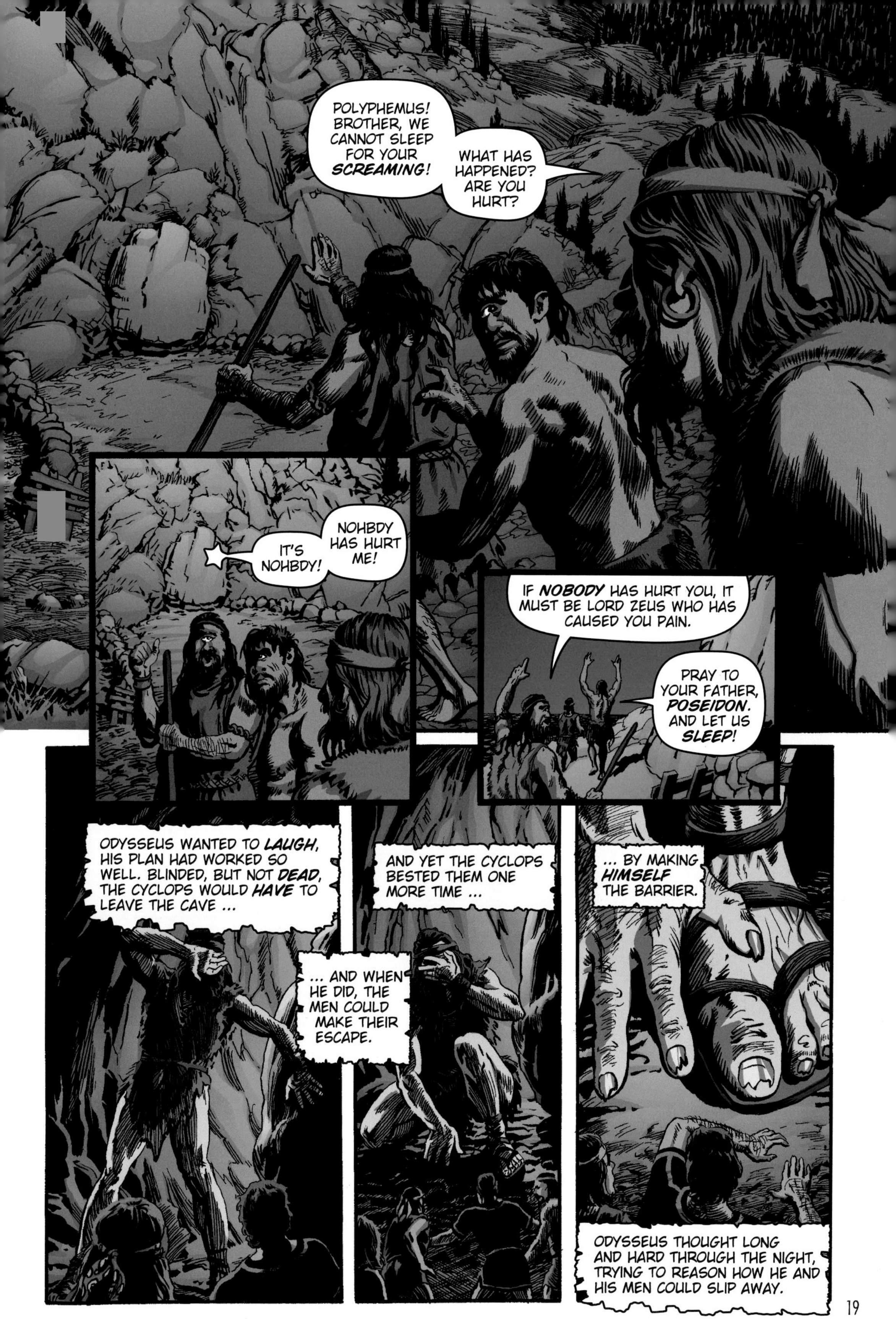
POLYPHEMUS! BROTHER, WE CANNOT SLEEP FOR YOUR SCREAMING!
WHAT HAS HAPPENED? ARE YOU HURT?
IT'S NOHBDY!
NOHBDY HAS HURT ME!
IF NOBODY HAS HURT YOU, IT MUST BE LORD ZEUS WHO HAS CAUSED YOU PAIN.
PRAY TO YOUR FATHER, POSEIDON. AND LET US SLEEP!
ODYSSEUS WANTED TO LAUGH, HIS PLAN HAD WORKED SO WELL. BLINDED, BUT NOT DEAD, THE CYCLOPS WOULD HAVE TO LEAVE THE CAVE ...
... AND WHEN HE DID, THE MEN COULD MAKE THEIR ESCAPE.
AND YET THE CYCLOPS BESTED THEM ONE MORE TIME ...
... BY MAKING HIMSELF THE BARRIER.
ODYSSEUS THOUGHT LONG AND HARD THROUGH THE NIGHT, TRYING TO REASON HOW HE AND HIS MEN COULD SLIP AWAY.

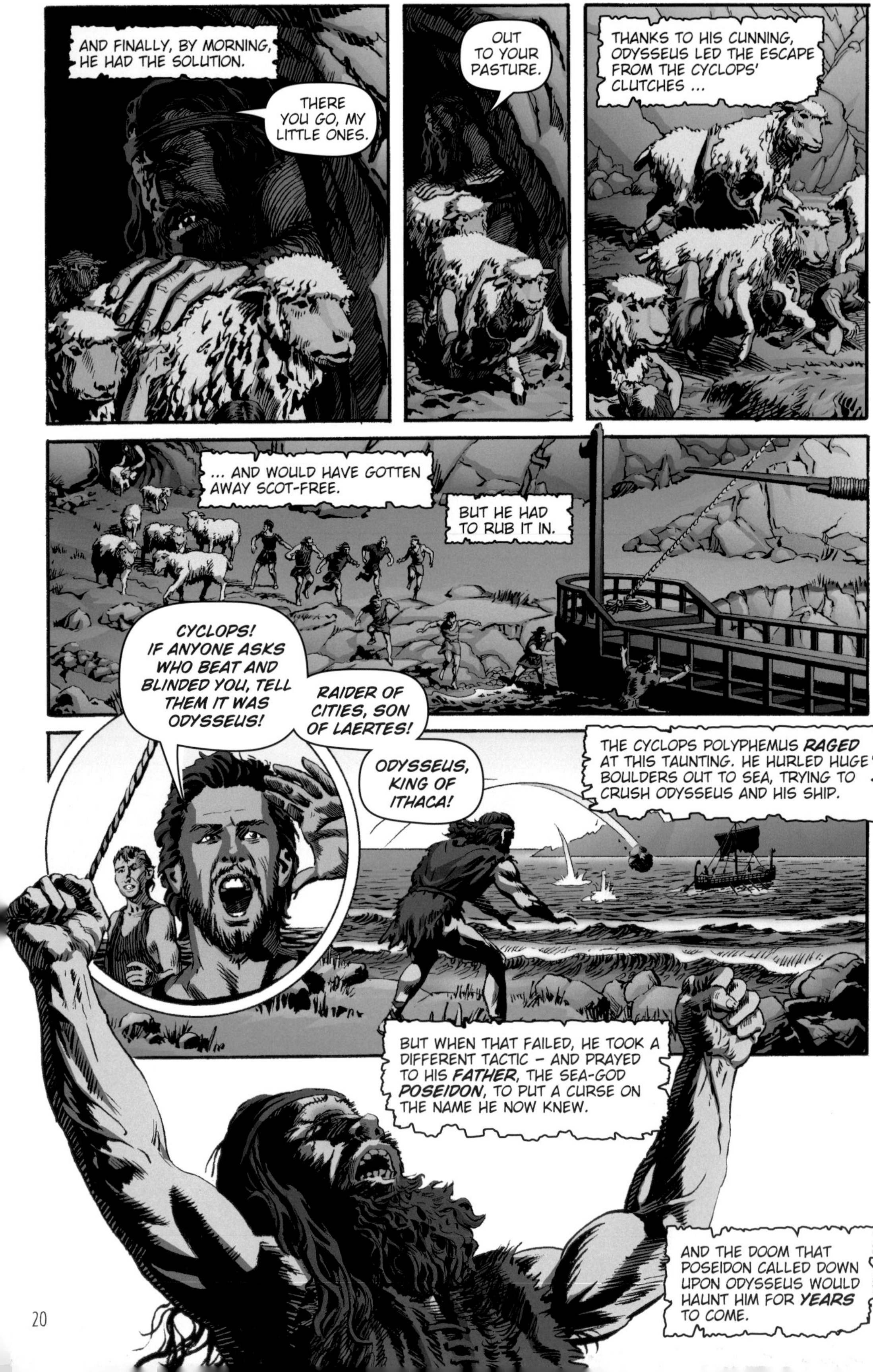

AND FINALLY, BY MORNING, HE HAD THE SOLUTION.
THERE YOU GO, MY LITTLE ONES.
OUT TO YOUR PASTURE.
THANKS TO HIS CUNNING, ODYSSEUS LED THE ESCAPE FROM THE CYCLOPS' CLUTCHES ...
... AND WOULD HAVE GOTTEN AWAY SCOT-FREE.
BUT HE HAD TO RUB IT IN.
CYCLOPS! IF ANYONE ASKS WHO BEAT AND BLINDED YOU, TELL THEM IT WAS ODYSSEUS!
RAIDER OF CITIES, SON OF LAERTES!
ODYSSEUS, KING OF ITHACA!
THE CYCLOPS POLYPHEMUS RAGED AT THIS TAUNTING. HE HURLED HUGE BOULDERS OUT TO SEA, TRYING TO CRUSH ODYSSEUS AND HIS SHIP.
BUT WHEN THAT FAILED, HE TOOK A DIFFERENT TACTIC – AND PRAYED TO HIS FATHER, THE SEA-GOD POSEIDON, TO PUT A CURSE ON THE NAME HE NOW KNEW.
AND THE DOOM THAT POSEIDON CALLED DOWN UPON ODYSSEUS WOULD HAUNT HIM FOR YEARS TO COME.

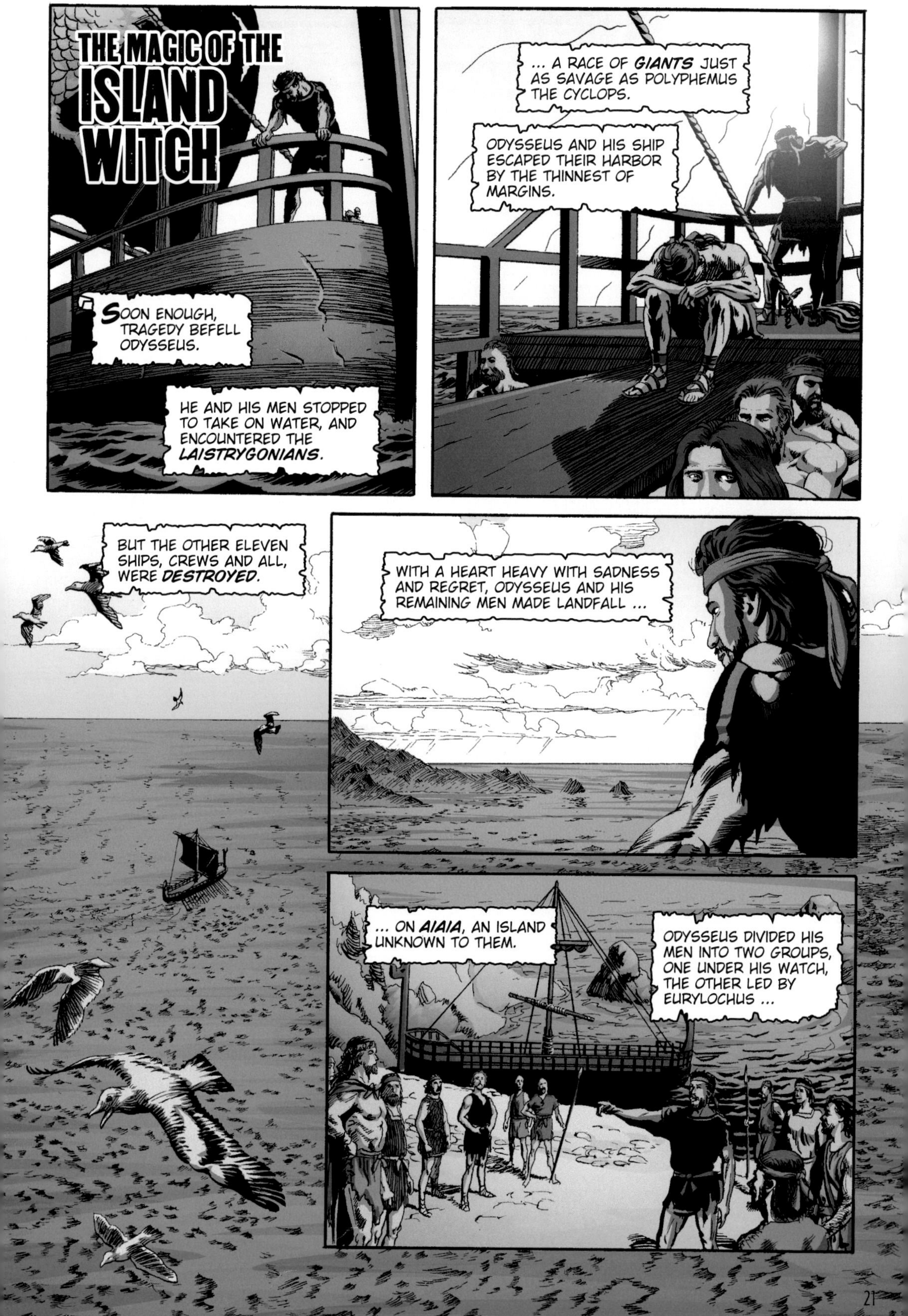
THE MAGIC OF THE ISLAND WITCH
SOON ENOUGH, TRAGEDY BEFELL ODYSSEUS.
HE AND HIS MEN STOPPED TO TAKE ON WATER, AND ENCOUNTERED THE LAISTRYGONIANS.
... A RACE OF GIANTS JUST AS SAVAGE AS POLYPHEMUS THE CYCLOPS.
ODYSSEUS AND HIS SHIP ESCAPED THEIR HARBOR BY THE THINNEST OF MARGINS.
BUT THE OTHER ELEVEN SHIPS, CREWS AND ALL, WERE DESTROYED.
WITH A HEART HEAVY WITH SADNESS AND REGRET, ODYSSEUS AND HIS REMAINING MEN MADE LANDFALL ...
... ON AIAIA, AN ISLAND UNKNOWN TO THEM.
ODYSSEUS DIVIDED HIS MEN INTO TWO GROUPS, ONE UNDER HIS WATCH, THE OTHER LED BY EURYLOCHUS ...

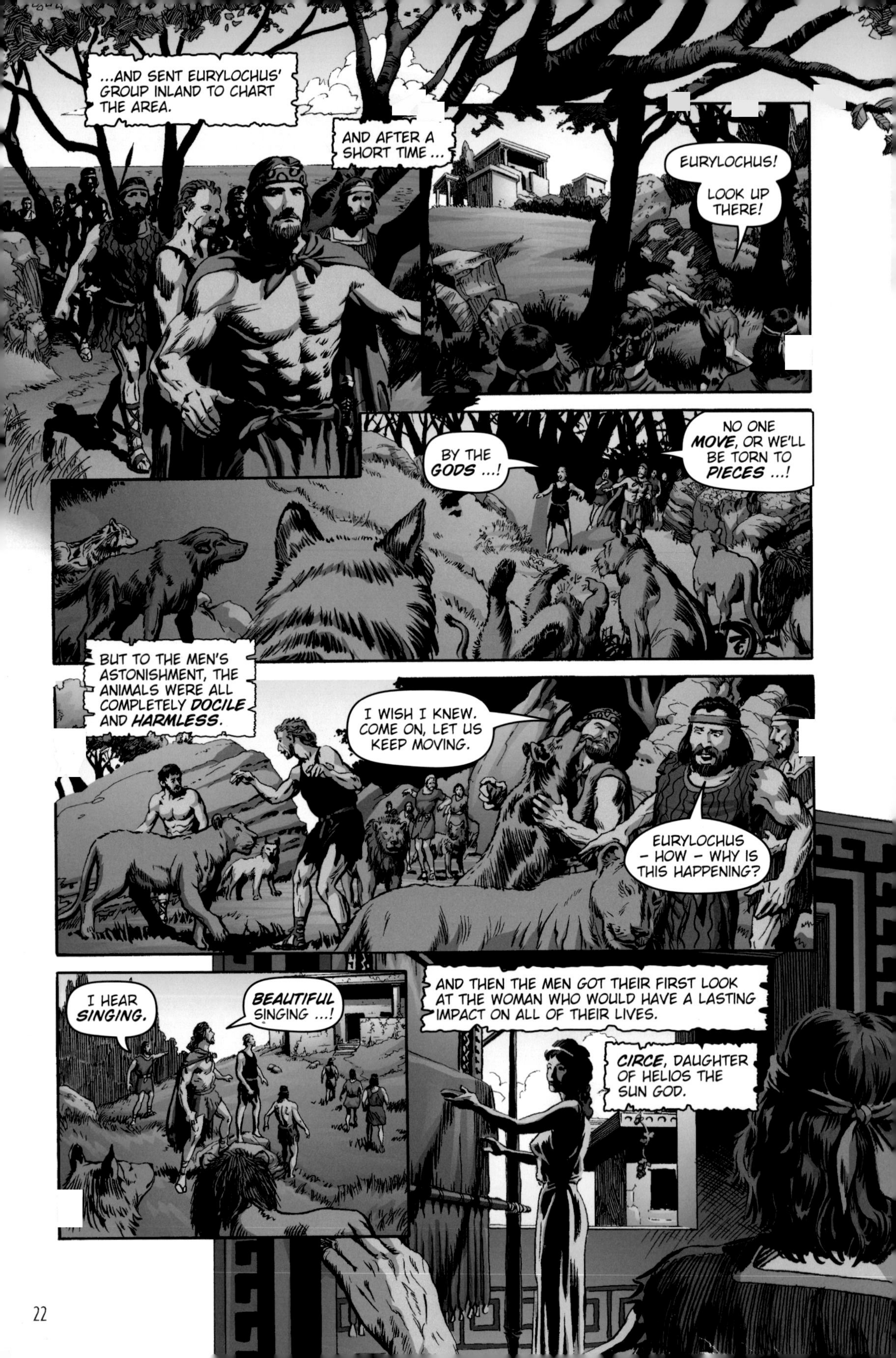

...AND SENT EURYLOCHUS' GROUP INLAND TO CHART THE AREA.
AND AFTER A SHORT TIME ...
EURYLOCHUS! LOOK UP THERE!
BY THE GODS ...!
NO ONE MOVE, OR WE'LL BE TORN TO PIECES ...!
BUT TO THE MEN'S ASTONISHMENT, THE ANIMALS WERE ALL COMPLETELY DOCILE AND HARMLESS.
EURYLOCHUS – HOW – WHY IS THIS HAPPENING?
I WISH I KNEW. COME ON, LET US KEEP MOVING.
I HEAR SINGING.
BEAUTIFUL SINGING ...!
AND THEN THE MEN GOT THEIR FIRST LOOK AT THE WOMAN WHO WOULD HAVE A LASTING IMPACT ON ALL OF THEIR LIVES.
CIRCE, DAUGHTER OF HELIOS THE SUN GOD.

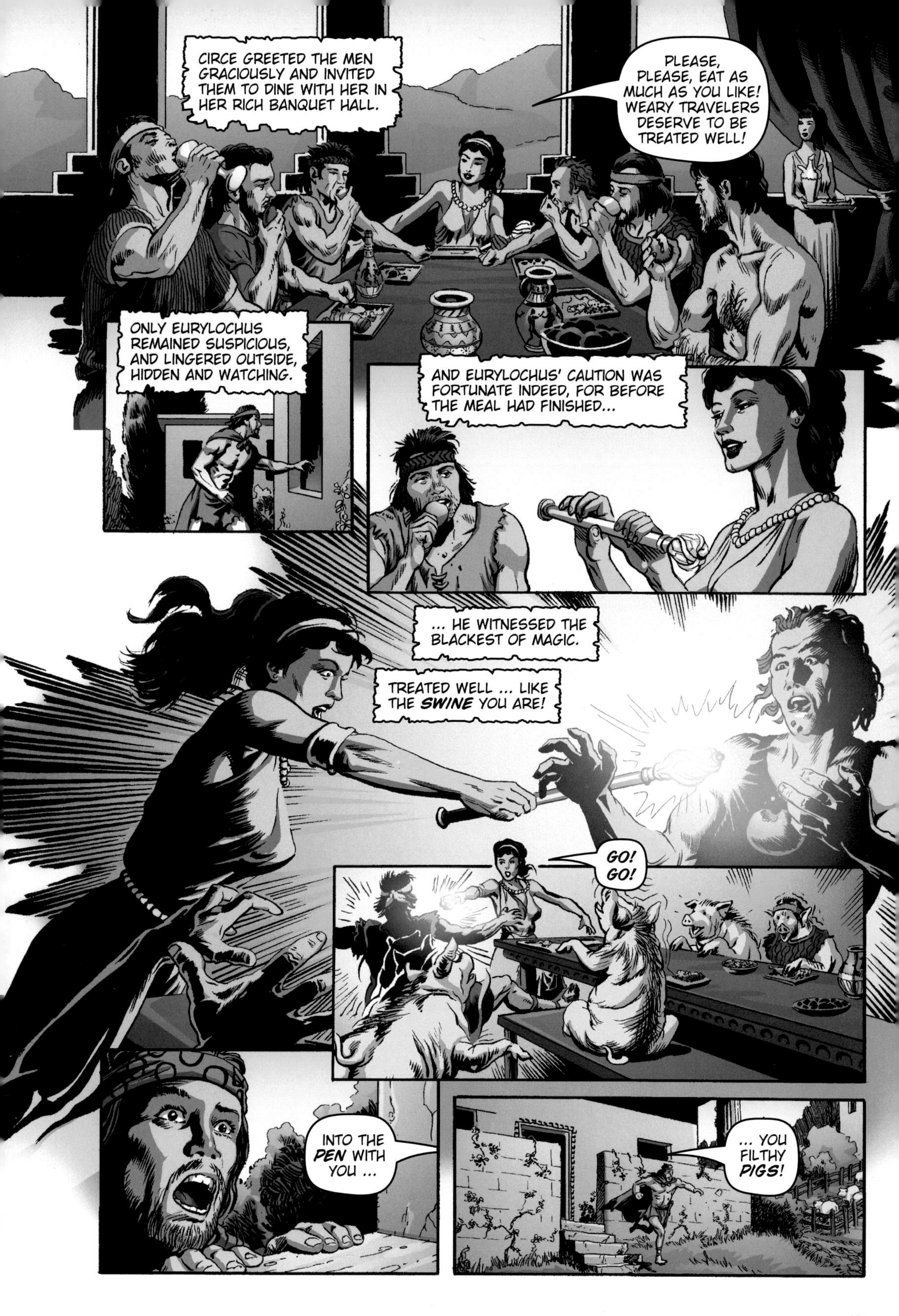
CIRCE GREETED THE MEN GRACIOUSLY AND INVITED THEM TO DINE WITH HER IN HER RICH BANQUET HALL.
PLEASE, PLEASE, EAT AS MUCH AS YOU LIKE! WEARY TRAVELERS DESERVE TO BE TREATED WELL!
ONLY EURYLOCHUS REMAINED SUSPICIOUS, AND LINGERED OUTSIDE, HIDDEN AND WATCHING.
AND EURYLOCHUS' CAUTION WAS FORTUNATE INDEED, FOR BEFORE THE MEAL HAD FINISHED...
... HE WITNESSED THE BLACKEST OF MAGIC.
TREATED WELL ... LIKE THE *SWINE* YOU ARE!
GO! GO!
INTO THE *PEN* WITH YOU ...
... YOU FILTHY *PIGS*!

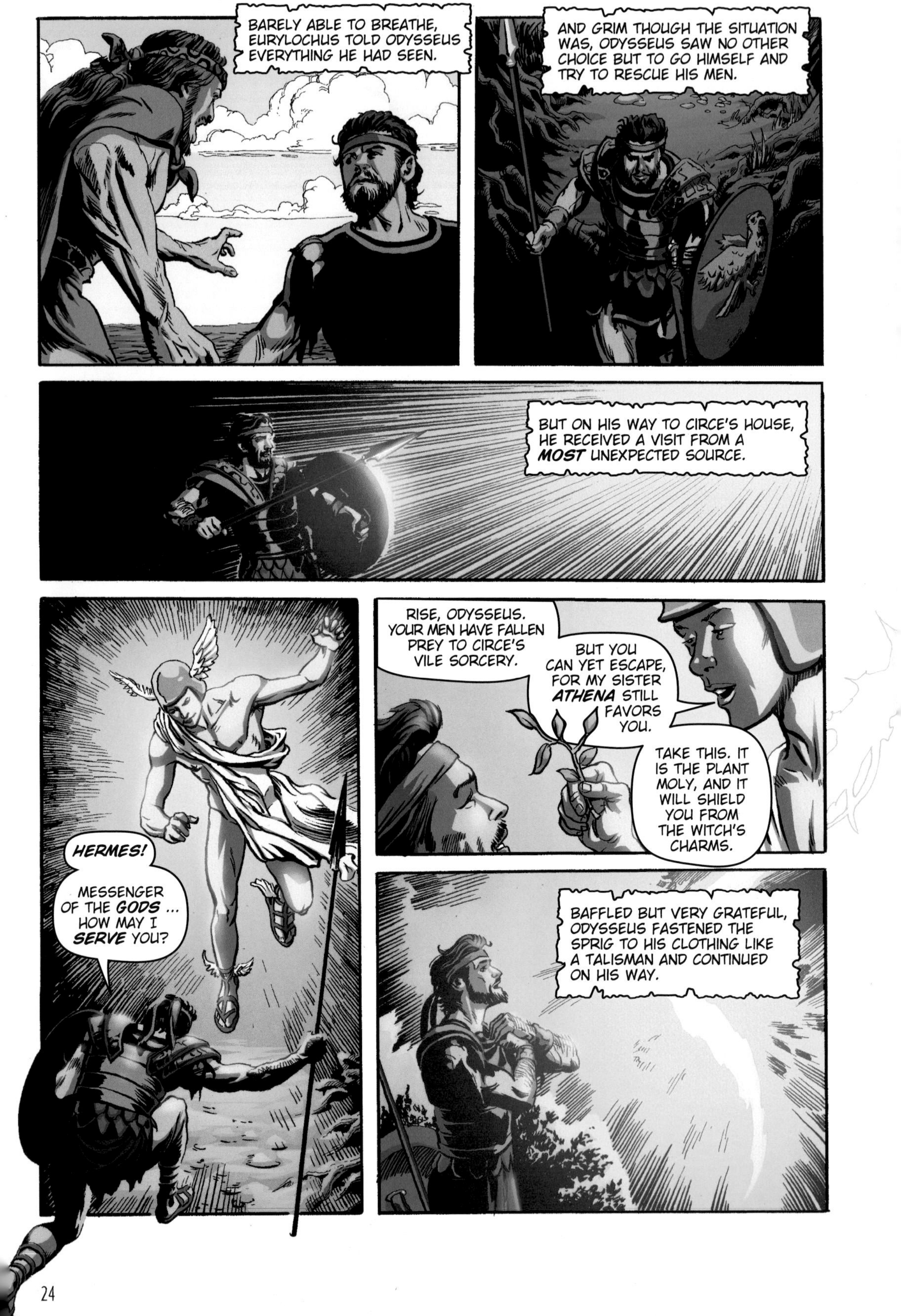
BARELY ABLE TO BREATHE, EURYLOCHUS TOLD ODYSSEUS EVERYTHING HE HAD SEEN.
AND GRIM THOUGH THE SITUATION WAS, ODYSSEUS SAW NO OTHER CHOICE BUT TO GO HIMSELF AND TRY TO RESCUE HIS MEN.
BUT ON HIS WAY TO CIRCE'S HOUSE, HE RECEIVED A VISIT FROM A MOST UNEXPECTED SOURCE.
HERMES!
MESSENGER OF THE GODS ... HOW MAY I SERVE YOU?
RISE, ODYSSEUS. YOUR MEN HAVE FALLEN PREY TO CIRCE'S VILE SORCERY.
BUT YOU CAN YET ESCAPE, FOR MY SISTER ATHENA STILL FAVORS YOU.
TAKE THIS. IT IS THE PLANT MOLY, AND IT WILL SHIELD YOU FROM THE WITCH'S CHARMS.
BAFFLED BUT VERY GRATEFUL, ODYSSEUS FASTENED THE SPRIG TO HIS CLOTHING LIKE A TALISMAN AND CONTINUED ON HIS WAY.

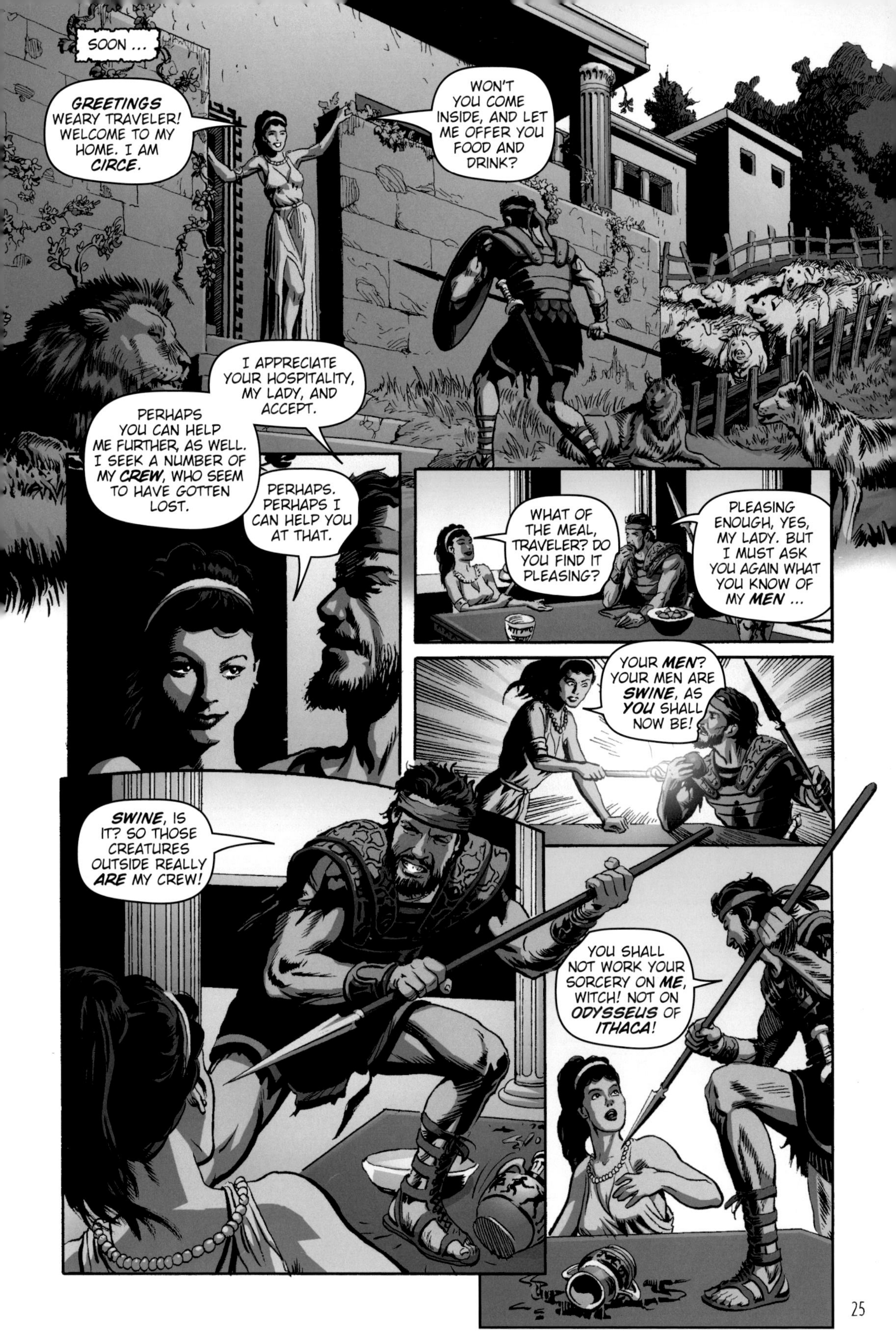
SOON ...
GREETINGS WEARY TRAVELER! WELCOME TO MY HOME. I AM CIRCE.
WON'T YOU COME INSIDE, AND LET ME OFFER YOU FOOD AND DRINK?
I APPRECIATE YOUR HOSPITALITY, MY LADY, AND ACCEPT.
PERHAPS YOU CAN HELP ME FURTHER, AS WELL. I SEEK A NUMBER OF MY CREW, WHO SEEM TO HAVE GOTTEN LOST.
PERHAPS. PERHAPS I CAN HELP YOU AT THAT.
WHAT OF THE MEAL, TRAVELER? DO YOU FIND IT PLEASING?
PLEASING ENOUGH, YES, MY LADY. BUT I MUST ASK YOU AGAIN WHAT YOU KNOW OF MY MEN ...
YOUR MEN? YOUR MEN ARE SWINE, AS YOU SHALL NOW BE!
SWINE, IS IT? SO THOSE CREATURES OUTSIDE REALLY ARE MY CREW!
YOU SHALL NOT WORK YOUR SORCERY ON ME, WITCH! NOT ON ODYSSEUS OF ITHACA!

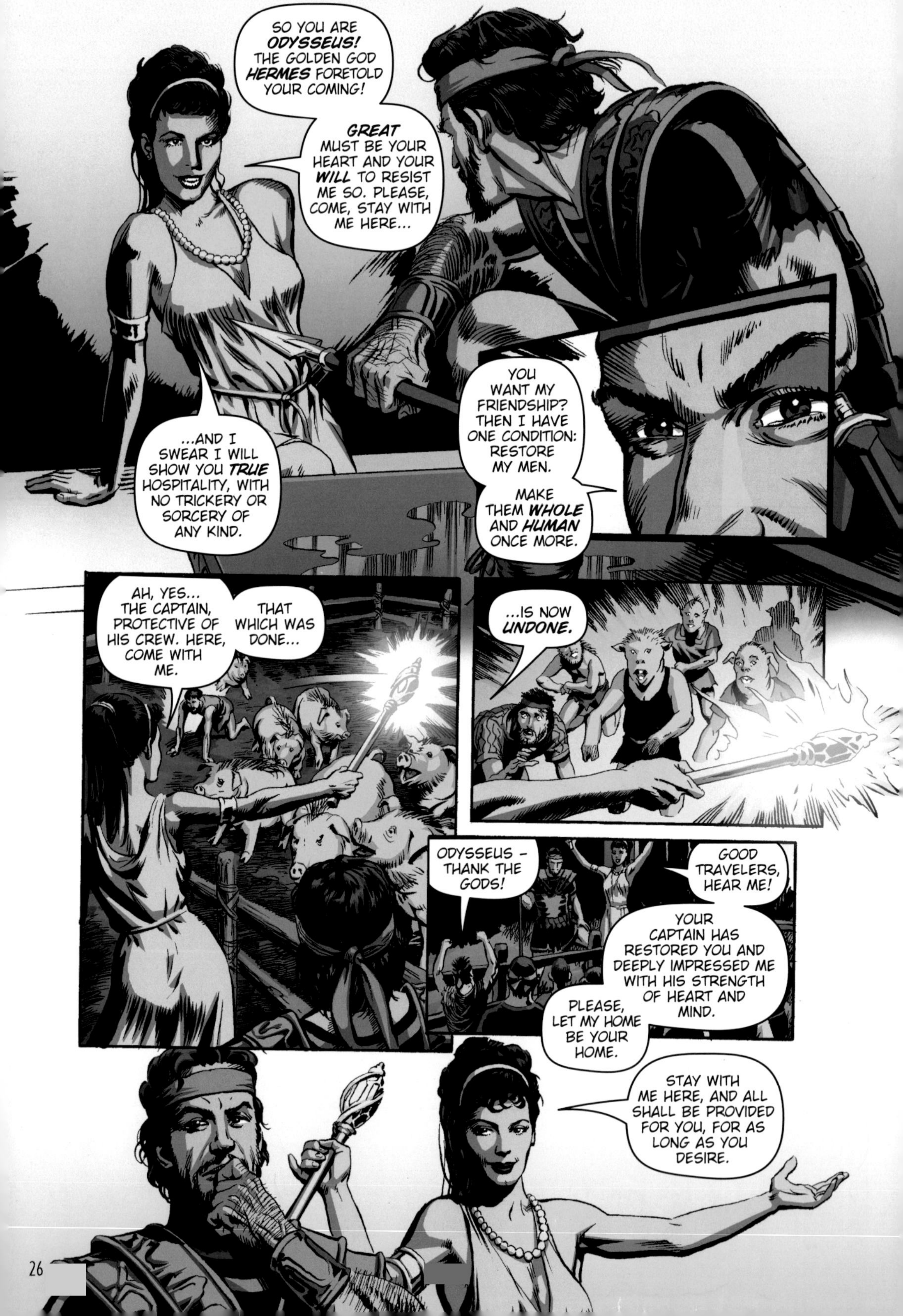
SO YOU ARE ODYSSEUS! THE GOLDEN GOD HERMES FORETOLD YOUR COMING!
GREAT MUST BE YOUR HEART AND YOUR WILL TO RESIST ME SO. PLEASE, COME, STAY WITH ME HERE...
...AND I SWEAR I WILL SHOW YOU TRUE HOSPITALITY, WITH NO TRICKERY OR SORCERY OF ANY KIND.
YOU WANT MY FRIENDSHIP? THEN I HAVE ONE CONDITION: RESTORE MY MEN.
MAKE THEM WHOLE AND HUMAN ONCE MORE.
AH, YES... THE CAPTAIN, PROTECTIVE OF HIS CREW. HERE, COME WITH ME.
THAT WHICH WAS DONE...
...IS NOW UNDONE.
ODYSSEUS - THANK THE GODS!
GOOD TRAVELERS, HEAR ME!
YOUR CAPTAIN HAS RESTORED YOU AND DEEPLY IMPRESSED ME WITH HIS STRENGTH OF HEART AND MIND.
PLEASE, LET MY HOME BE YOUR HOME.
STAY WITH ME HERE, AND ALL SHALL BE PROVIDED FOR YOU, FOR AS LONG AS YOU DESIRE.

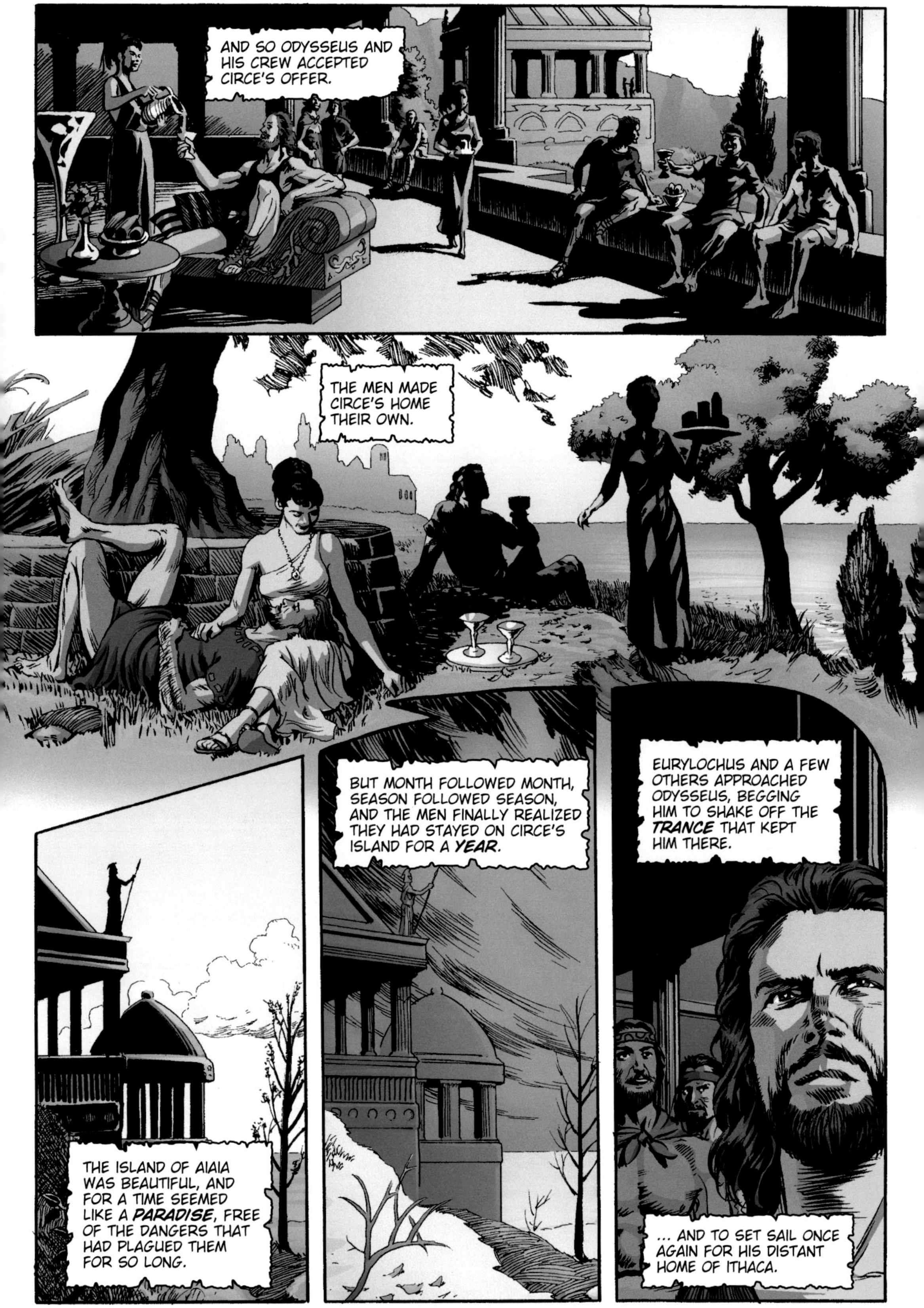
AND SO ODYSSEUS AND HIS CREW ACCEPTED CIRCE'S OFFER.
THE MEN MADE CIRCE'S HOME THEIR OWN.
THE ISLAND OF AIAIA WAS BEAUTIFUL, AND FOR A TIME SEEMED LIKE A PARADISE, FREE OF THE DANGERS THAT HAD PLAGUED THEM FOR SO LONG.
BUT MONTH FOLLOWED MONTH, SEASON FOLLOWED SEASON, AND THE MEN FINALLY REALIZED THEY HAD STAYED ON CIRCE'S ISLAND FOR A YEAR.
EURYLOCHUS AND A FEW OTHERS APPROACHED ODYSSEUS, BEGGING HIM TO SHAKE OFF THE TRANCE THAT KEPT HIM THERE.
... AND TO SET SAIL ONCE AGAIN FOR HIS DISTANT HOME OF ITHACA.

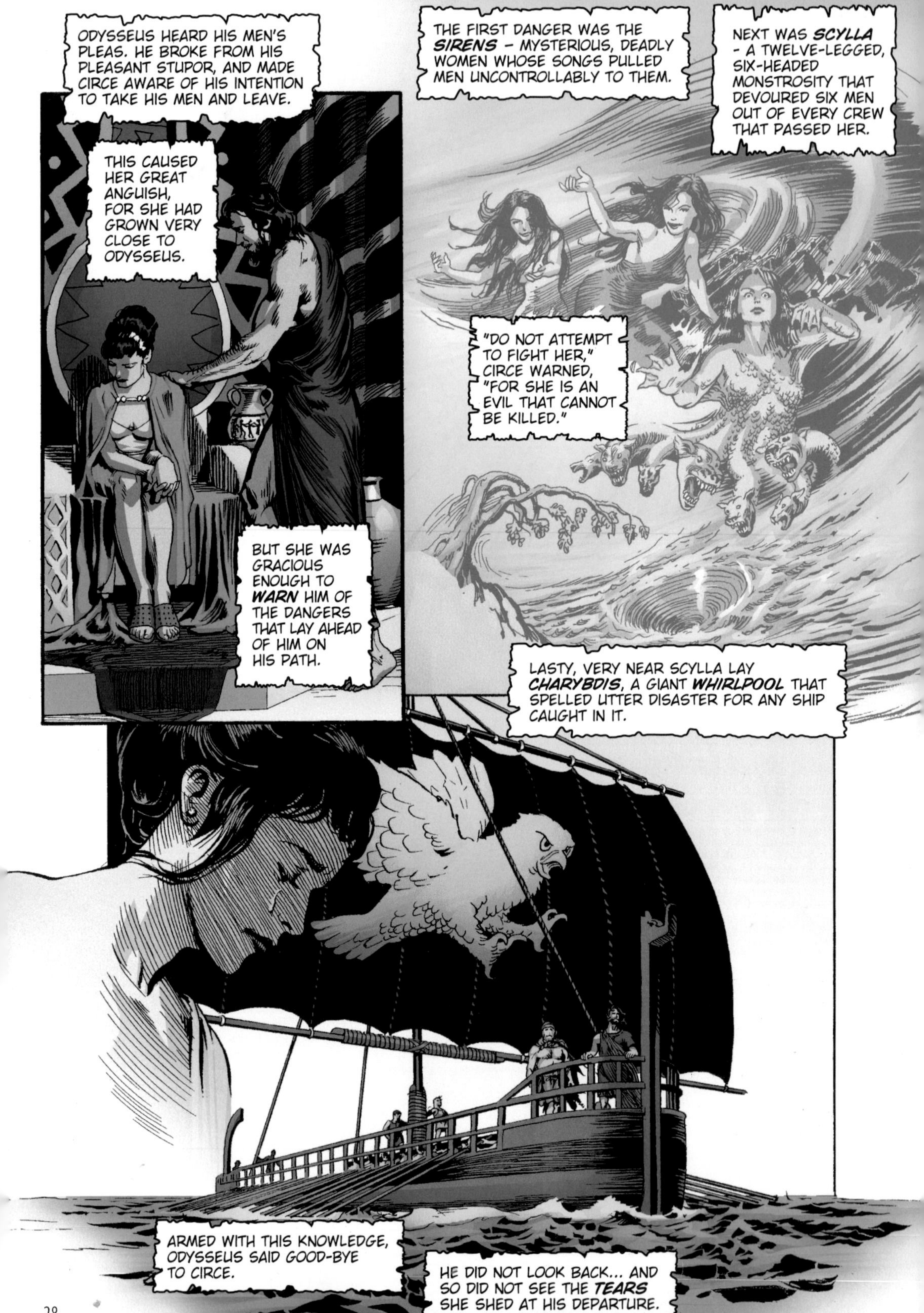
ODYSSEUS HEARD HIS MEN'S PLEAS. HE BROKE FROM HIS PLEASANT STUPOR, AND MADE CIRCE AWARE OF HIS INTENTION TO TAKE HIS MEN AND LEAVE.
THIS CAUSED HER GREAT ANGUISH, FOR SHE HAD GROWN VERY CLOSE TO ODYSSEUS.
BUT SHE WAS GRACIOUS ENOUGH TO WARN HIM OF THE DANGERS THAT LAY AHEAD OF HIM ON HIS PATH.
THE FIRST DANGER WAS THE SIRENS – MYSTERIOUS, DEADLY WOMEN WHOSE SONGS PULLED MEN UNCONTROLLABLY TO THEM.
NEXT WAS SCYLLA - A TWELVE-LEGGED, SIX-HEADED MONSTROSITY THAT DEVOURED SIX MEN OUT OF EVERY CREW THAT PASSED HER.
"DO NOT ATTEMPT TO FIGHT HER," CIRCE WARNED, "FOR SHE IS AN EVIL THAT CANNOT BE KILLED."
LASTY, VERY NEAR SCYLLA LAY CHARYBDIS, A GIANT WHIRLPOOL THAT SPELLED UTTER DISASTER FOR ANY SHIP CAUGHT IN IT.
ARMED WITH THIS KNOWLEDGE, ODYSSEUS SAID GOOD-BYE TO CIRCE.
HE DID NOT LOOK BACK... AND SO DID NOT SEE THE TEARS SHE SHED AT HIS DEPARTURE.

AN ORDEAL OF MONSTERS

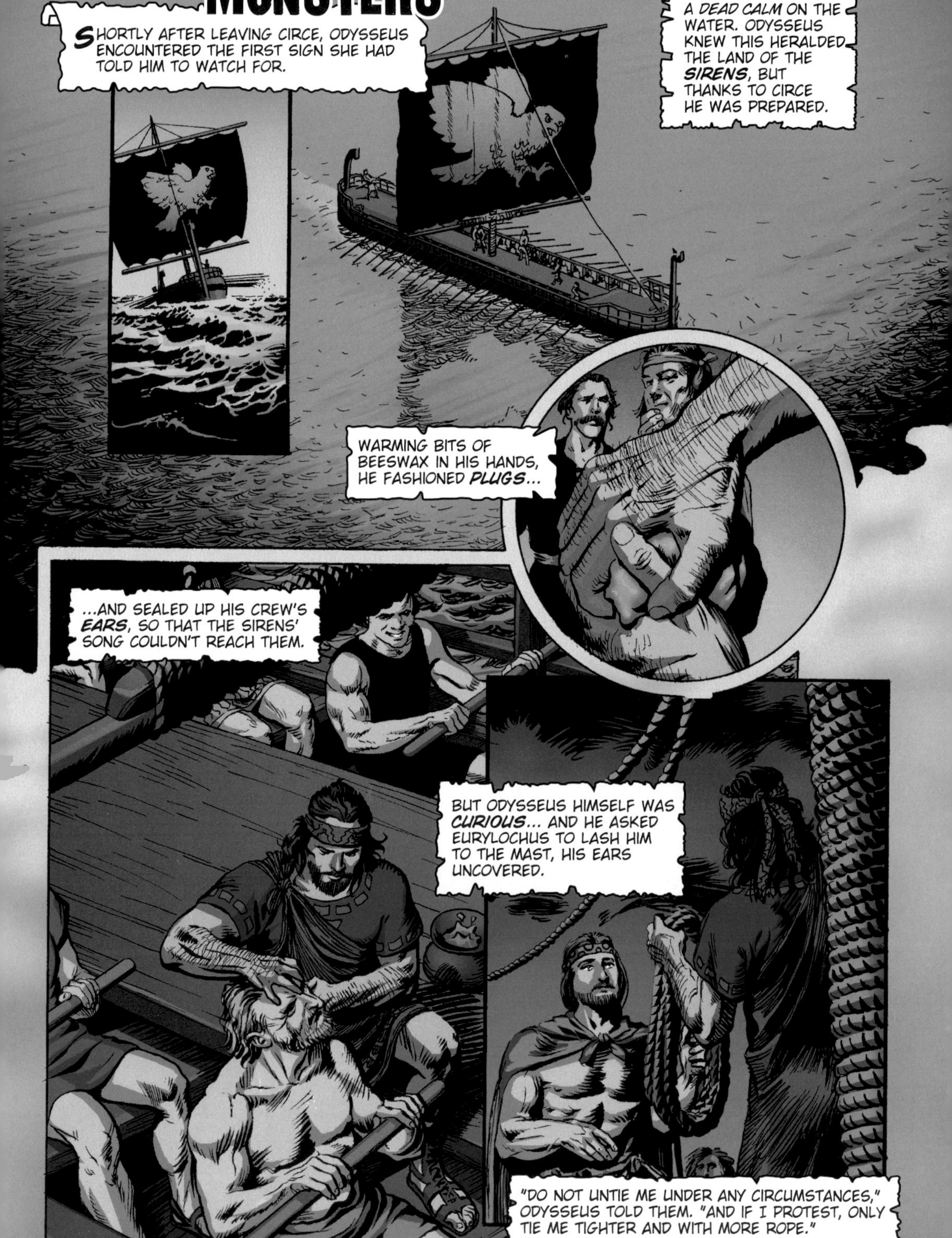
SHORTLY AFTER LEAVING CIRCE, ODYSSEUS ENCOUNTERED THE FIRST SIGN SHE HAD TOLD HIM TO WATCH FOR.
A DEAD CALM ON THE WATER. ODYSSEUS KNEW THIS HERALDED THE LAND OF THE SIRENS, BUT THANKS TO CIRCE HE WAS PREPARED.
WARMING BITS OF BEESWAX IN HIS HANDS, HE FASHIONED PLUGS...
...AND SEALED UP HIS CREW'S EARS, SO THAT THE SIRENS' SONG COULDN'T REACH THEM.
BUT ODYSSEUS HIMSELF WAS CURIOUS... AND HE ASKED EURYLOCHUS TO LASH HIM TO THE MAST, HIS EARS UNCOVERED.
"DO NOT UNTIE ME UNDER ANY CIRCUMSTANCES," ODYSSEUS TOLD THEM. "AND IF I PROTEST, ONLY TIE ME TIGHTER AND WITH MORE ROPE."

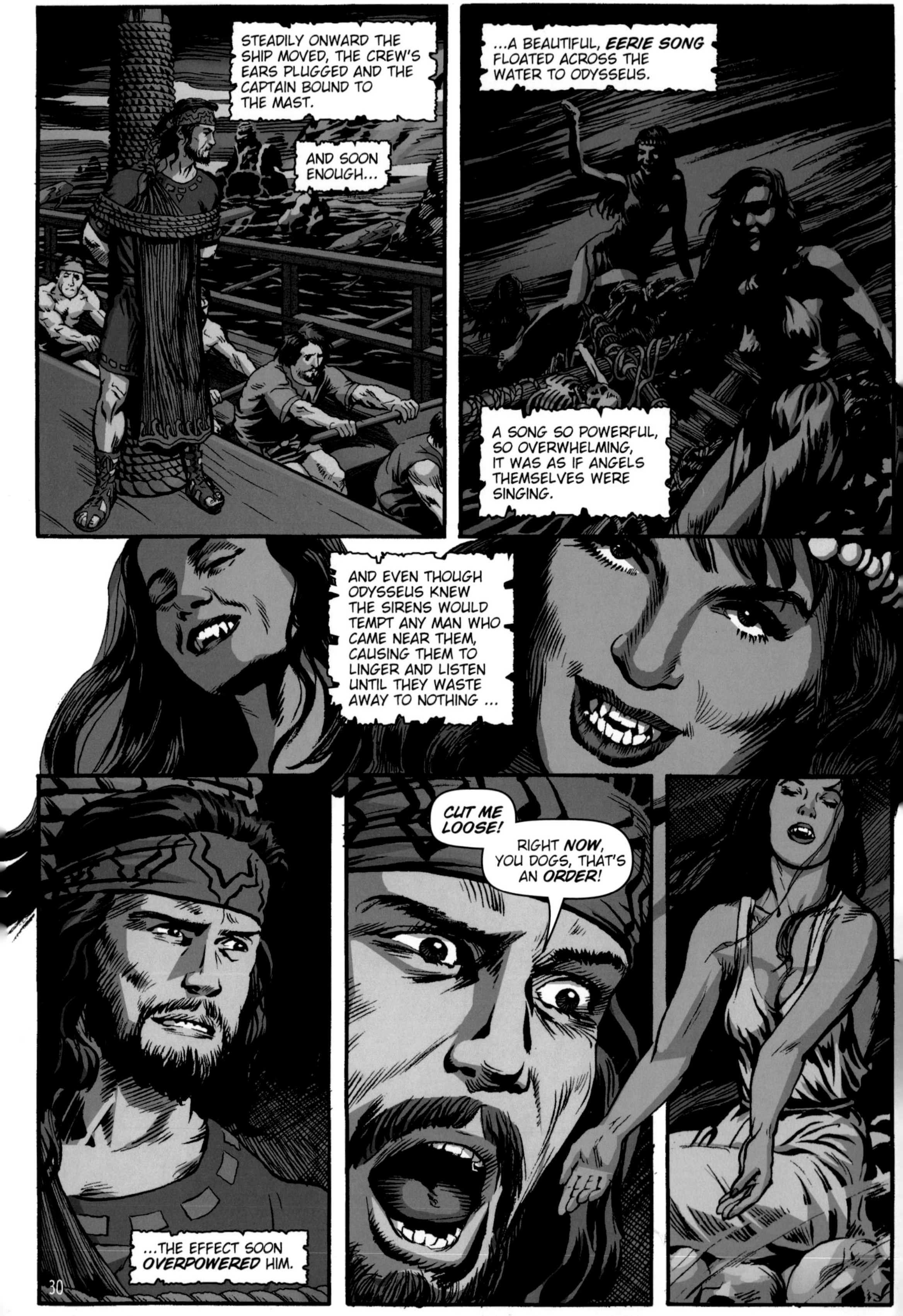
STEADILY ONWARD THE SHIP MOVED, THE CREW'S EARS PLUGGED AND THE CAPTAIN BOUND TO THE MAST.
AND SOON ENOUGH...
...A BEAUTIFUL, EERIE SONG FLOATED ACROSS THE WATER TO ODYSSEUS.
A SONG SO POWERFUL, SO OVERWHELMING, IT WAS AS IF ANGELS THEMSELVES WERE SINGING.
AND EVEN THOUGH ODYSSEUS KNEW THE SIRENS WOULD TEMPT ANY MAN WHO CAME NEAR THEM, CAUSING THEM TO LINGER AND LISTEN UNTIL THEY WASTE AWAY TO NOTHING ...
...THE EFFECT SOON OVERPOWERED HIM.
CUT ME LOOSE!
RIGHT NOW, YOU DOGS, THAT'S AN ORDER!

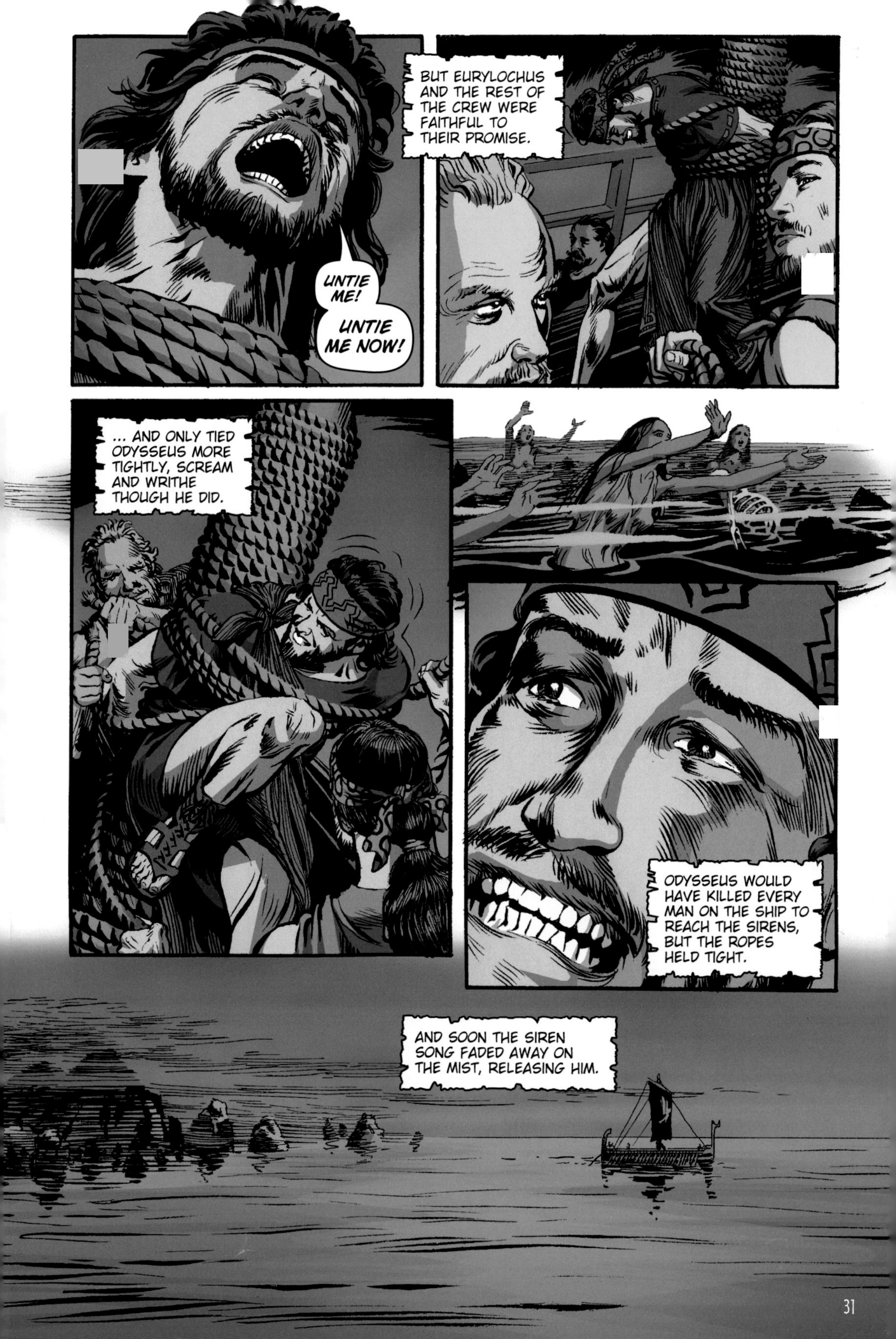
UNTIE ME!
UNTIE ME NOW!
BUT EURYLOCHUS AND THE REST OF THE CREW WERE FAITHFUL TO THEIR PROMISE.
... AND ONLY TIED ODYSSEUS MORE TIGHTLY, SCREAM AND WRITHE THOUGH HE DID.
ODYSSEUS WOULD HAVE KILLED EVERY MAN ON THE SHIP TO REACH THE SIRENS, BUT THE ROPES HELD TIGHT.
AND SOON THE SIREN SONG FADED AWAY ON THE MIST, RELEASING HIM.

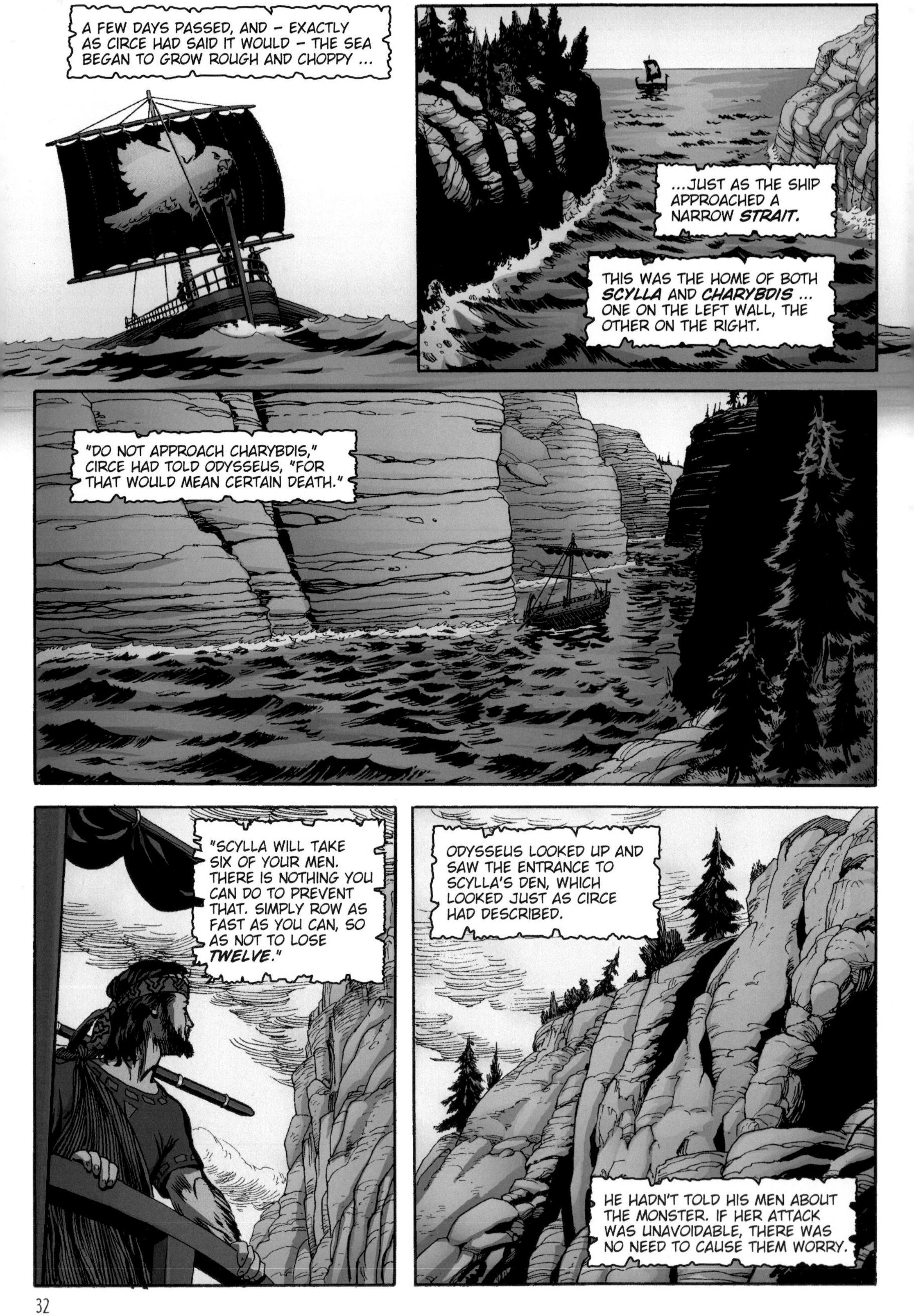
A FEW DAYS PASSED, AND – EXACTLY AS CIRCE HAD SAID IT WOULD – THE SEA BEGAN TO GROW ROUGH AND CHOPPY ...
...JUST AS THE SHIP APPROACHED A NARROW STRAIT.
THIS WAS THE HOME OF BOTH SCYLLA AND CHARYBDIS ... ONE ON THE LEFT WALL, THE OTHER ON THE RIGHT.
"DO NOT APPROACH CHARYBDIS," CIRCE HAD TOLD ODYSSEUS, "FOR THAT WOULD MEAN CERTAIN DEATH."
"SCYLLA WILL TAKE SIX OF YOUR MEN. THERE IS NOTHING YOU CAN DO TO PREVENT THAT. SIMPLY ROW AS FAST AS YOU CAN, SO AS NOT TO LOSE TWELVE."
ODYSSEUS LOOKED UP AND SAW THE ENTRANCE TO SCYLLA'S DEN, WHICH LOOKED JUST AS CIRCE HAD DESCRIBED.
HE HADN'T TOLD HIS MEN ABOUT THE MONSTER. IF HER ATTACK WAS UNAVOIDABLE, THERE WAS NO NEED TO CAUSE THEM WORRY.

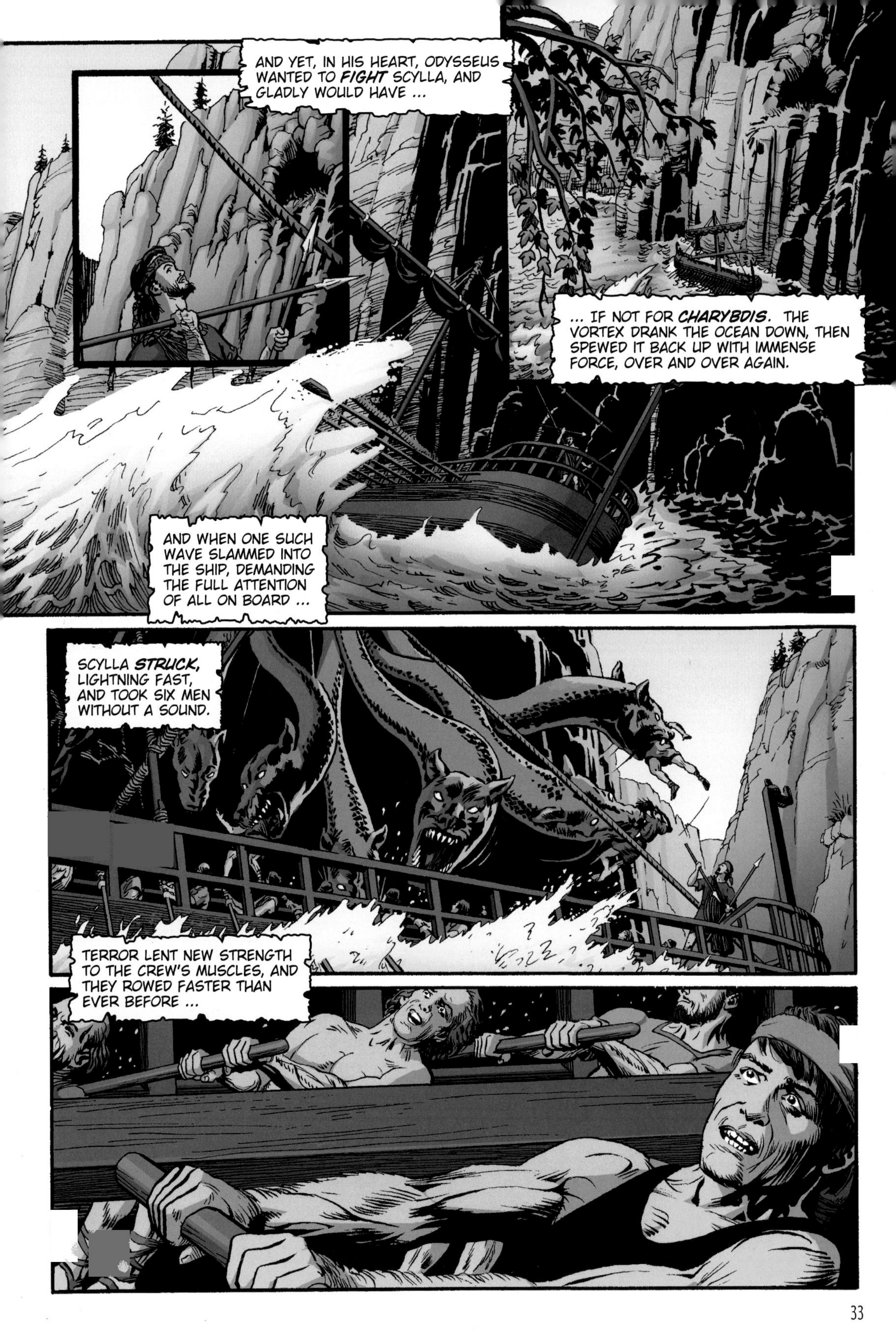
AND YET, IN HIS HEART, ODYSSEUS WANTED TO FIGHT SCYLLA, AND GLADLY WOULD HAVE ...
... IF NOT FOR CHARYBDIS. THE VORTEX DRANK THE OCEAN DOWN, THEN SPEWED IT BACK UP WITH IMMENSE FORCE, OVER AND OVER AGAIN.
AND WHEN ONE SUCH WAVE SLAMMED INTO THE SHIP, DEMANDING THE FULL ATTENTION OF ALL ON BOARD ...
SCYLLA STRUCK, LIGHTNING FAST, AND TOOK SIX MEN WITHOUT A SOUND.
TERROR LENT NEW STRENGTH TO THE CREW'S MUSCLES, AND THEY ROWED FASTER THAN EVER BEFORE ...

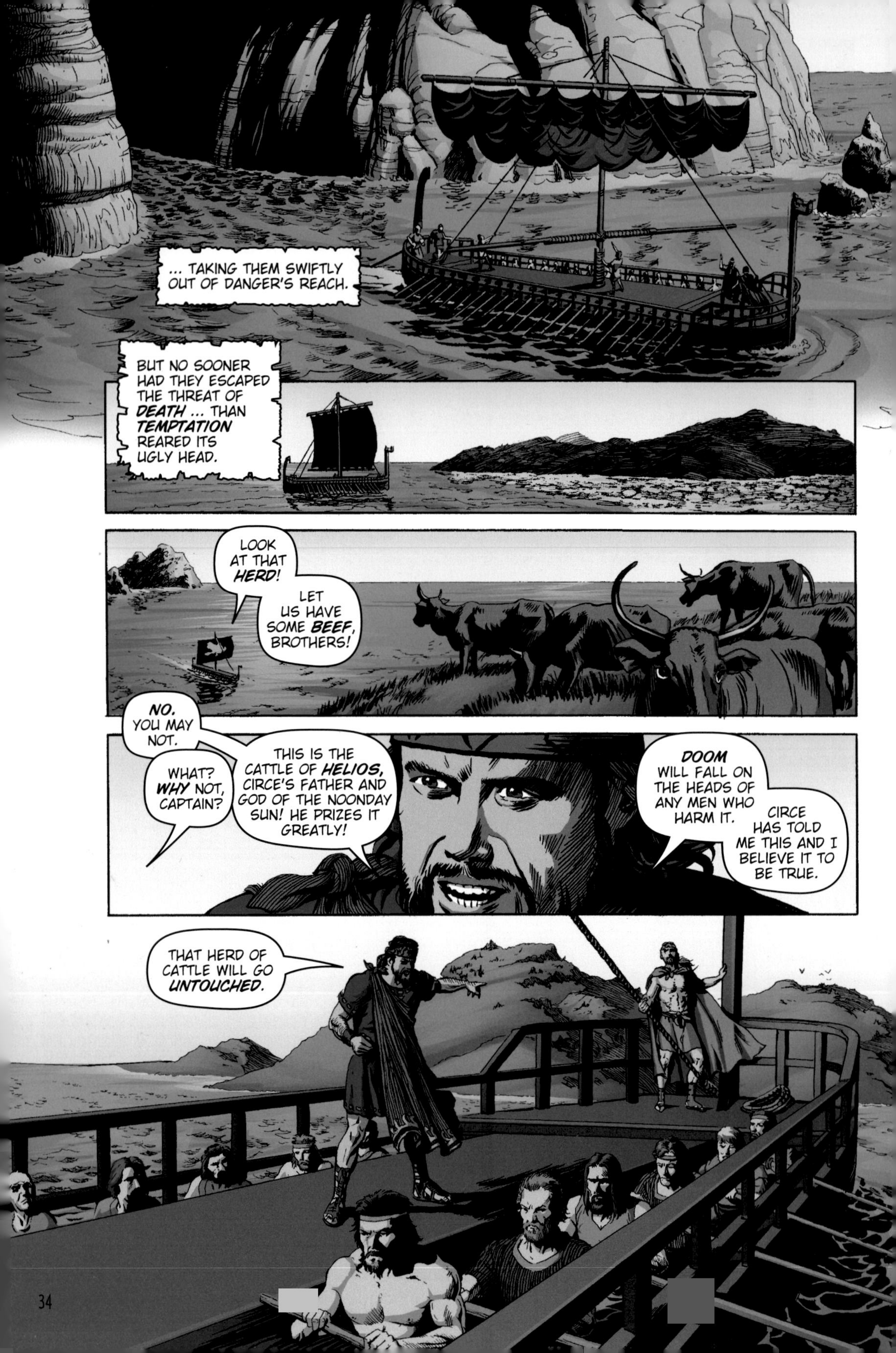
... TAKING THEM SWIFTLY OUT OF DANGER'S REACH.
BUT NO SOONER HAD THEY ESCAPED THE THREAT OF DEATH ... THAN TEMPTATION REARED ITS UGLY HEAD.
LOOK AT THAT HERD!
LET US HAVE SOME BEEF, BROTHERS!
NO. YOU MAY NOT.
WHAT? WHY NOT, CAPTAIN?
THIS IS THE CATTLE OF HELIOS, CIRCE'S FATHER AND GOD OF THE NOONDAY SUN! HE PRIZES IT GREATLY!
DOOM WILL FALL ON THE HEADS OF ANY MEN WHO HARM IT.
CIRCE HAS TOLD ME THIS AND I BELIEVE IT TO BE TRUE.
THAT HERD OF CATTLE WILL GO UNTOUCHED.

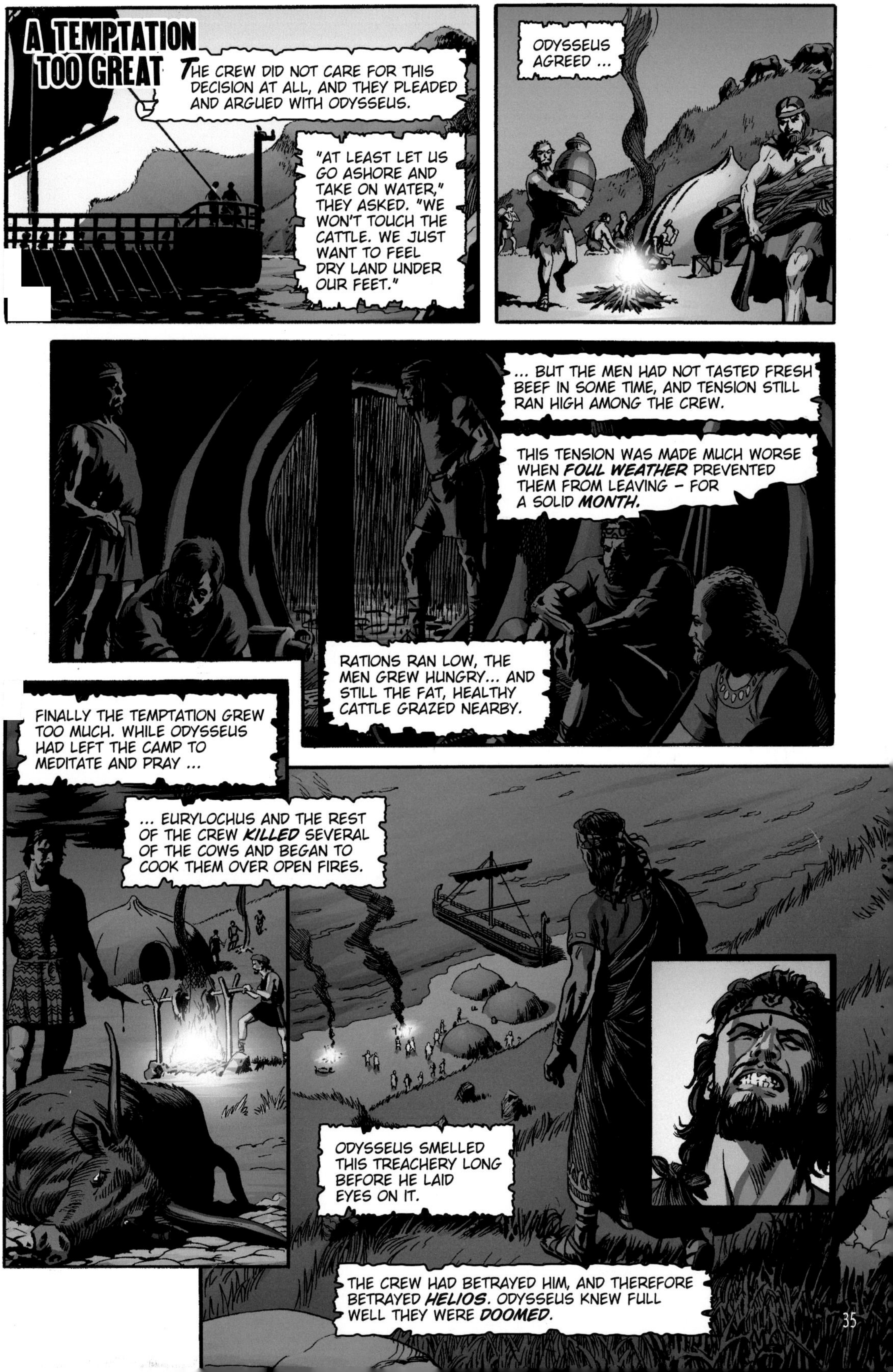
A TEMPTATION TOO GREAT
THE CREW DID NOT CARE FOR THIS DECISION AT ALL, AND THEY PLEADED AND ARGUED WITH ODYSSEUS.
"AT LEAST LET US GO ASHORE AND TAKE ON WATER," THEY ASKED. "WE WON'T TOUCH THE CATTLE. WE JUST WANT TO FEEL DRY LAND UNDER OUR FEET."
ODYSSEUS AGREED ...
... BUT THE MEN HAD NOT TASTED FRESH BEEF IN SOME TIME, AND TENSION STILL RAN HIGH AMONG THE CREW.
THIS TENSION WAS MADE MUCH WORSE WHEN FOUL WEATHER PREVENTED THEM FROM LEAVING - FOR A SOLID MONTH.
RATIONS RAN LOW, THE MEN GREW HUNGRY... AND STILL THE FAT, HEALTHY CATTLE GRAZED NEARBY.
FINALLY THE TEMPTATION GREW TOO MUCH. WHILE ODYSSEUS HAD LEFT THE CAMP TO MEDITATE AND PRAY ...
... EURYLOCHUS AND THE REST OF THE CREW KILLED SEVERAL OF THE COWS AND BEGAN TO COOK THEM OVER OPEN FIRES.
ODYSSEUS SMELLED THIS TREACHERY LONG BEFORE HE LAID EYES ON IT.
THE CREW HAD BETRAYED HIM, AND THEREFORE BETRAYED HELIOS. ODYSSEUS KNEW FULL WELL THEY WERE DOOMED.

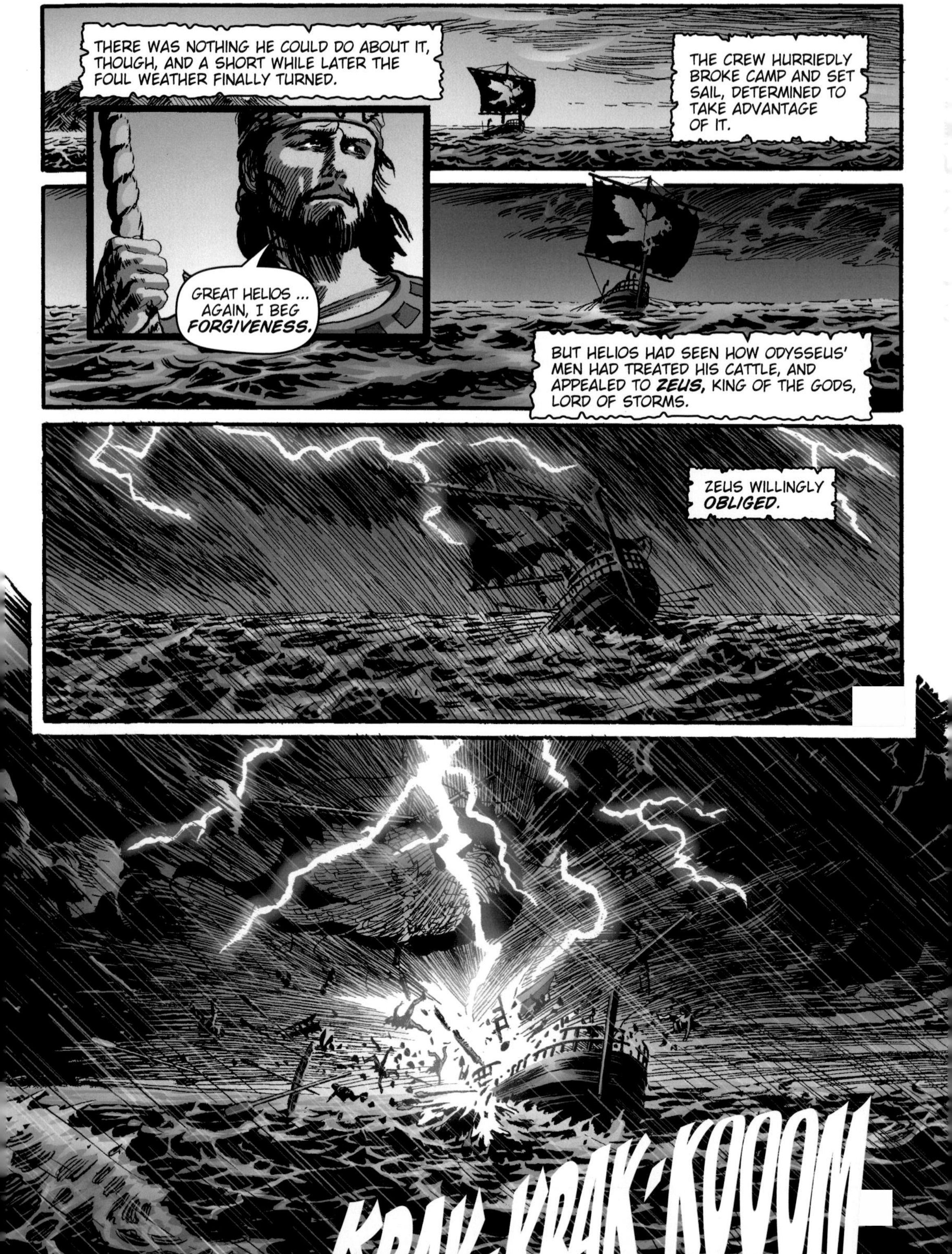
THERE WAS NOTHING HE COULD DO ABOUT IT, THOUGH, AND A SHORT WHILE LATER THE FOUL WEATHER FINALLY TURNED.
THE CREW HURRIEDLY BROKE CAMP AND SET SAIL, DETERMINED TO TAKE ADVANTAGE OF IT.
GREAT HELIOS ... AGAIN, I BEG **FORGIVENESS.**
BUT HELIOS HAD SEEN HOW ODYSSEUS' MEN HAD TREATED HIS CATTLE, AND APPEALED TO **ZEUS,** KING OF THE GODS, LORD OF STORMS.
ZEUS WILLINGLY **OBLIGED.**
KRAK-KRAK-KOOOM

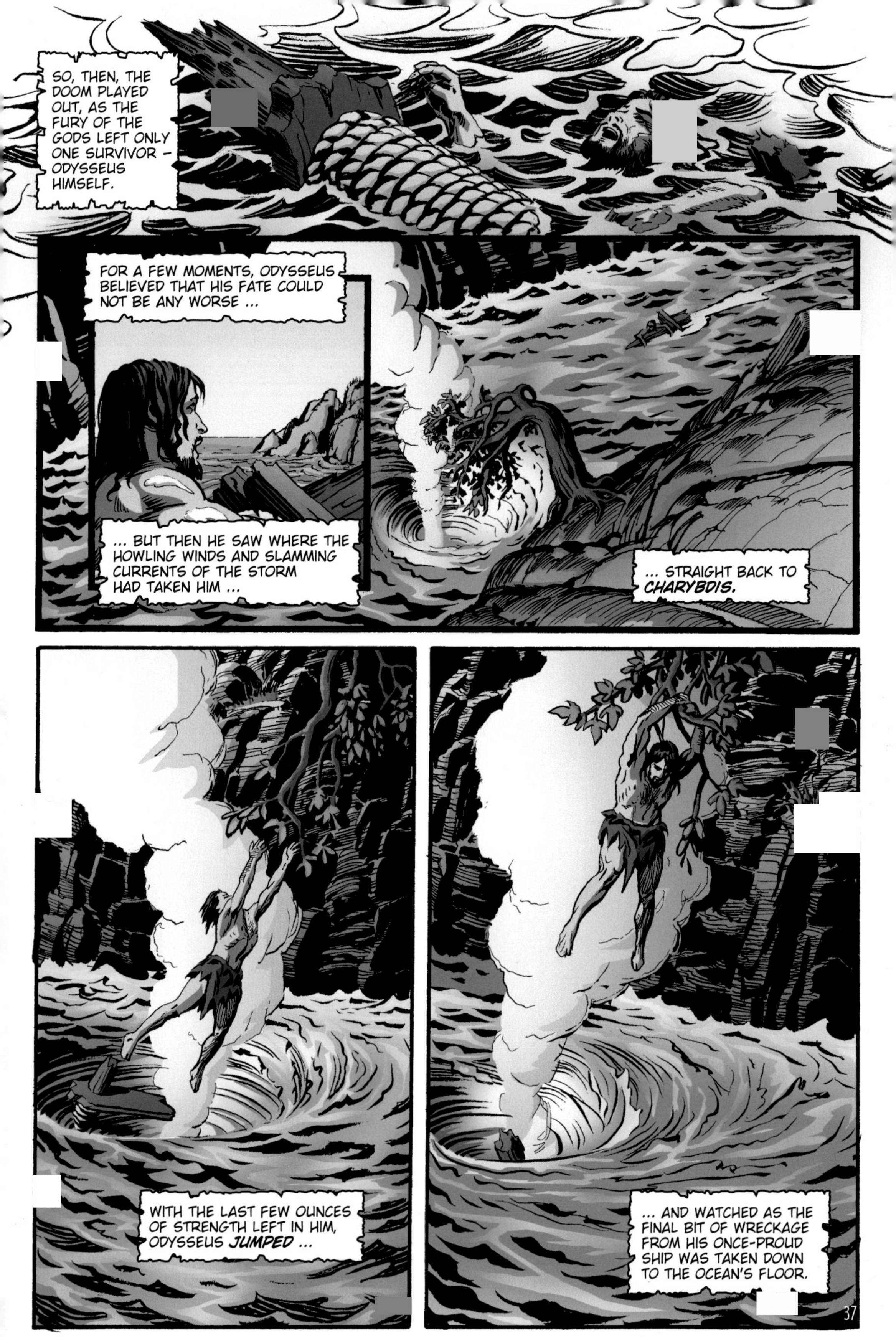
SO, THEN, THE DOOM PLAYED OUT, AS THE FURY OF THE GODS LEFT ONLY ONE SURVIVOR – ODYSSEUS HIMSELF.
FOR A FEW MOMENTS, ODYSSEUS BELIEVED THAT HIS FATE COULD NOT BE ANY WORSE ...
... BUT THEN HE SAW WHERE THE HOWLING WINDS AND SLAMMING CURRENTS OF THE STORM HAD TAKEN HIM ...
... STRAIGHT BACK TO CHARYBDIS.
WITH THE LAST FEW OUNCES OF STRENGTH LEFT IN HIM, ODYSSEUS JUMPED ...
... AND WATCHED AS THE FINAL BIT OF WRECKAGE FROM HIS ONCE-PROUD SHIP WAS TAKEN DOWN TO THE OCEAN'S FLOOR.

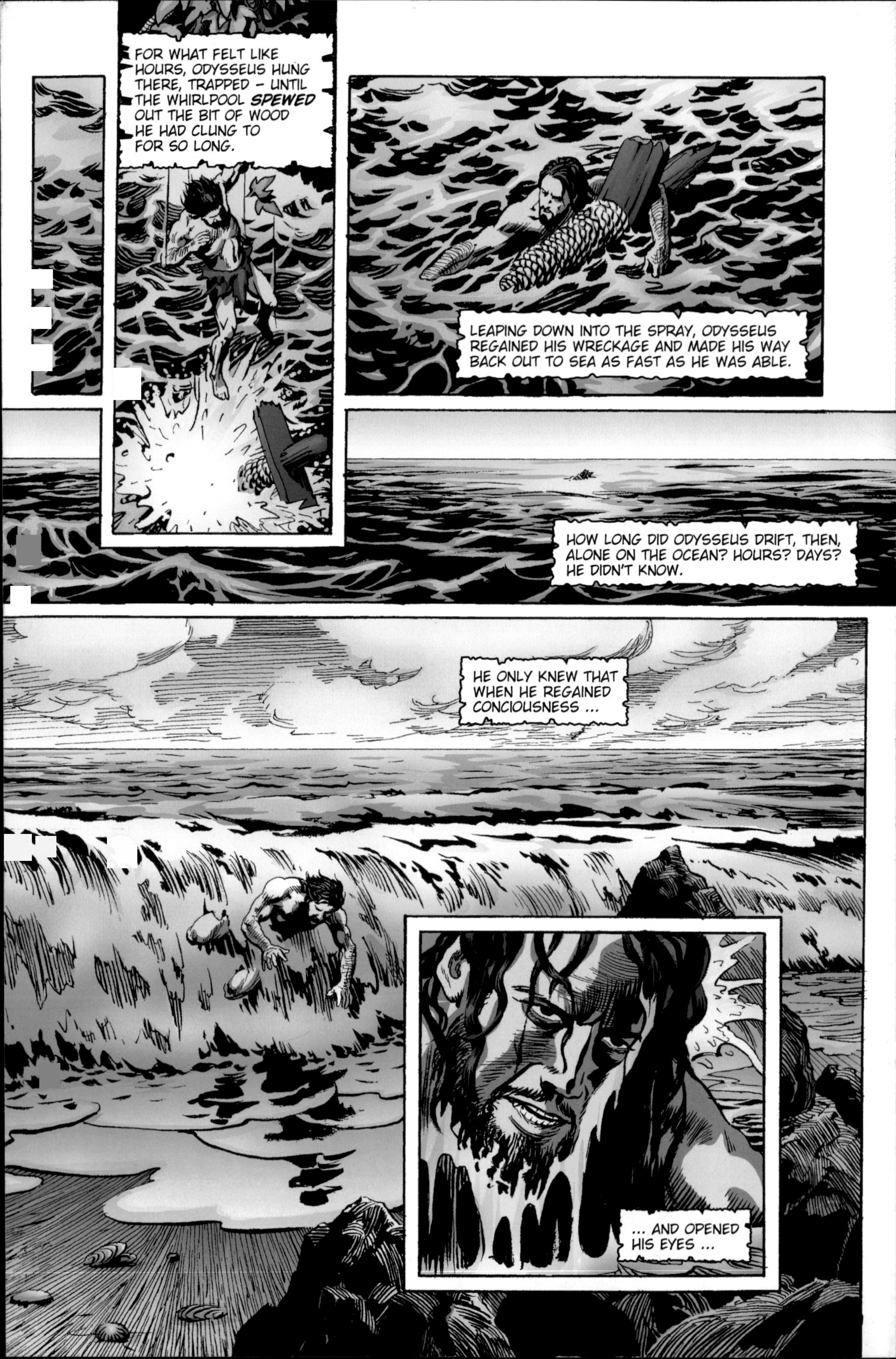
FOR WHAT FELT LIKE HOURS, ODYSSEUS HUNG THERE, TRAPPED – UNTIL THE WHIRLPOOL SPEWED OUT THE BIT OF WOOD HE HAD CLUNG TO FOR SO LONG.
LEAPING DOWN INTO THE SPRAY, ODYSSEUS REGAINED HIS WRECKAGE AND MADE HIS WAY BACK OUT TO SEA AS FAST AS HE WAS ABLE.
HOW LONG DID ODYSSEUS DRIFT, THEN, ALONE ON THE OCEAN? HOURS? DAYS? HE DIDN'T KNOW.
HE ONLY KNEW THAT WHEN HE REGAINED CONCIOUSNESS ...
... AND OPENED HIS EYES ...

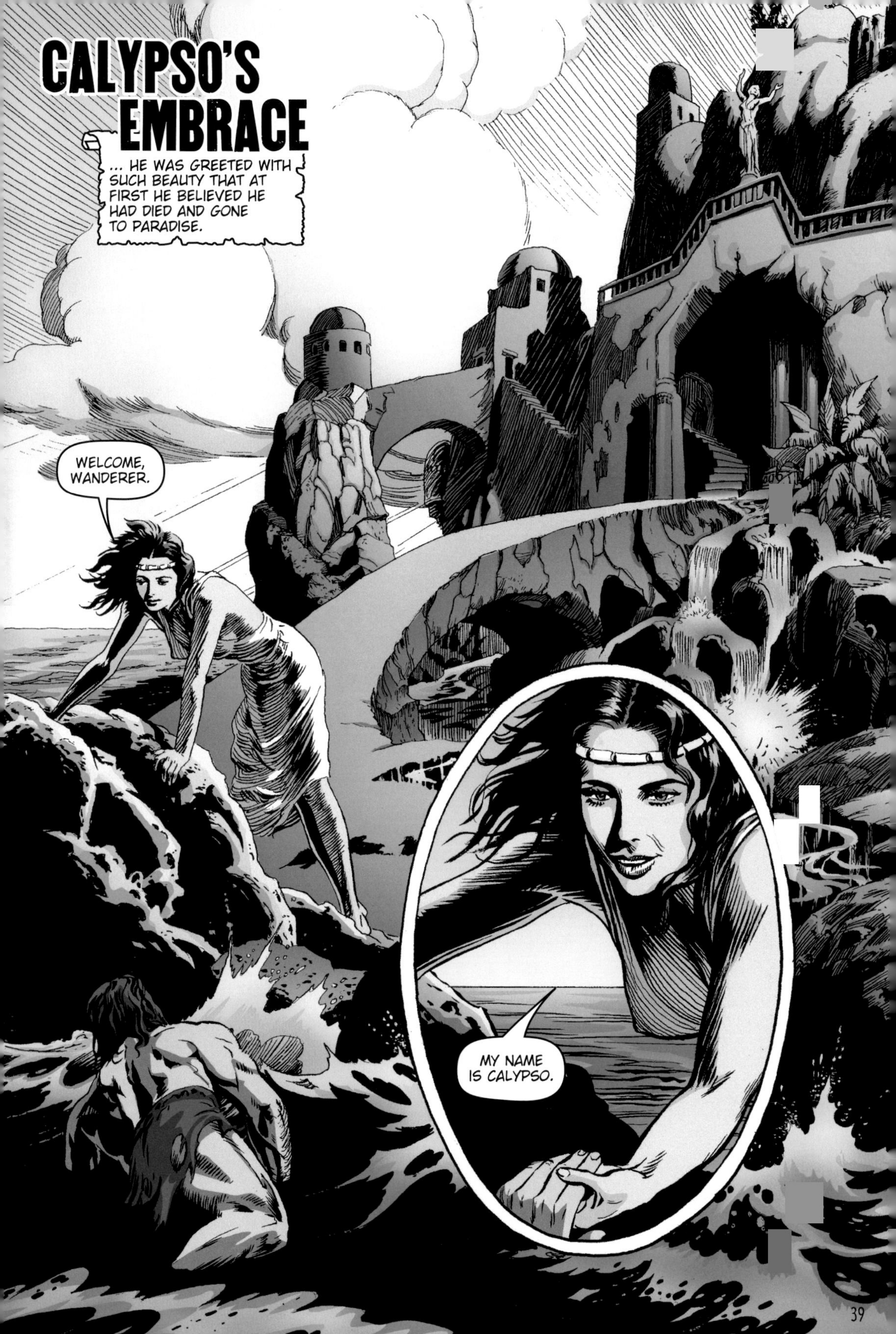
CALYPSO'S EMBRACE
... HE WAS GREETED WITH SUCH BEAUTY THAT AT FIRST HE BELIEVED HE HAD DIED AND GONE TO PARADISE.
WELCOME, WANDERER.
MY NAME IS CALYPSO.

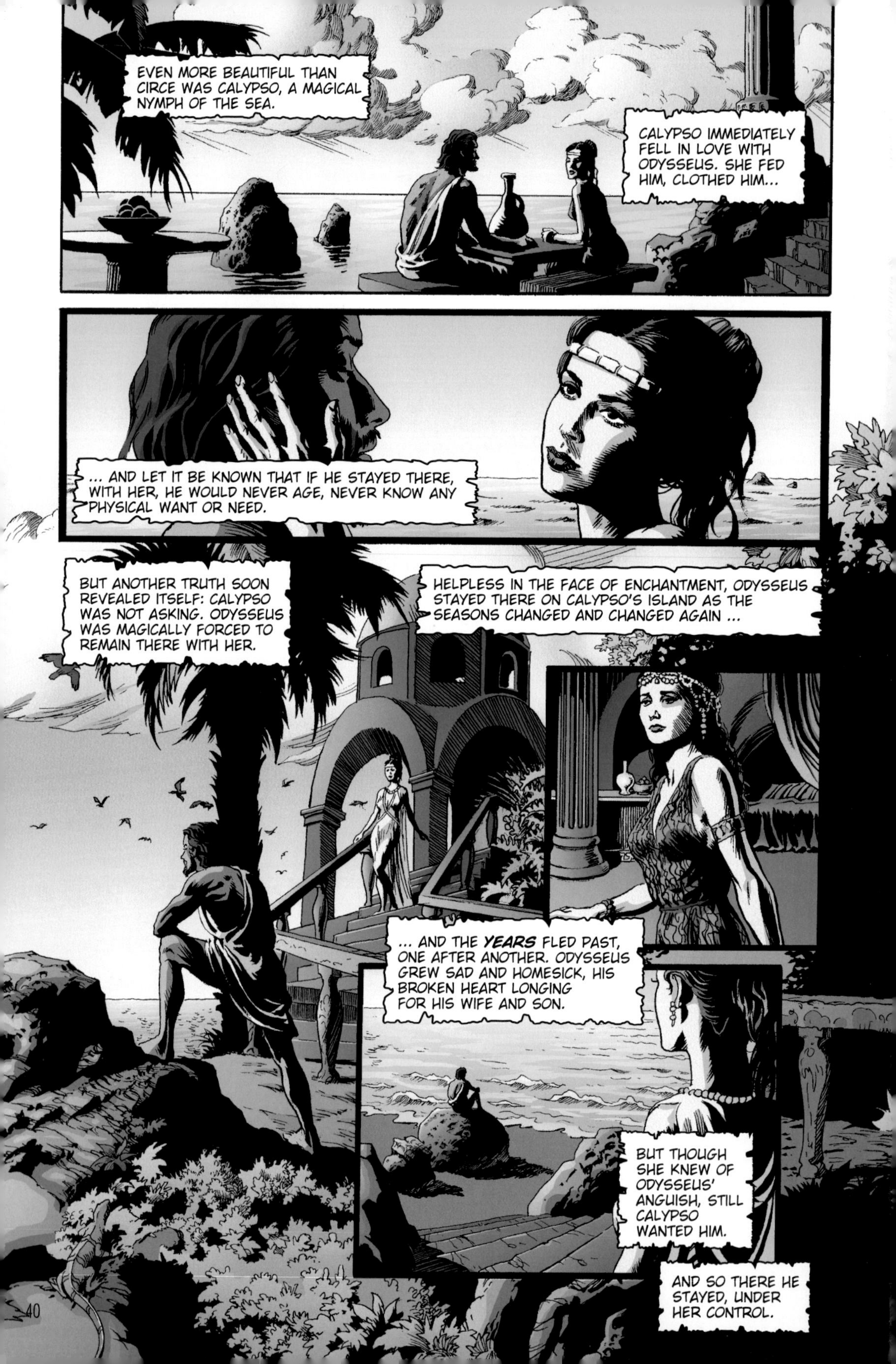
EVEN MORE BEAUTIFUL THAN CIRCE WAS CALYPSO, A MAGICAL NYMPH OF THE SEA.
CALYPSO IMMEDIATELY FELL IN LOVE WITH ODYSSEUS. SHE FED HIM, CLOTHED HIM...
... AND LET IT BE KNOWN THAT IF HE STAYED THERE, WITH HER, HE WOULD NEVER AGE, NEVER KNOW ANY PHYSICAL WANT OR NEED.
BUT ANOTHER TRUTH SOON REVEALED ITSELF: CALYPSO WAS NOT ASKING. ODYSSEUS WAS MAGICALLY FORCED TO REMAIN THERE WITH HER.
HELPLESS IN THE FACE OF ENCHANTMENT, ODYSSEUS STAYED THERE ON CALYPSO'S ISLAND AS THE SEASONS CHANGED AND CHANGED AGAIN ...
... AND THE *YEARS* FLED PAST, ONE AFTER ANOTHER. ODYSSEUS GREW SAD AND HOMESICK, HIS BROKEN HEART LONGING FOR HIS WIFE AND SON.
BUT THOUGH SHE KNEW OF ODYSSEUS' ANGUISH, STILL CALYPSO WANTED HIM.
AND SO THERE HE STAYED, UNDER HER CONTROL.

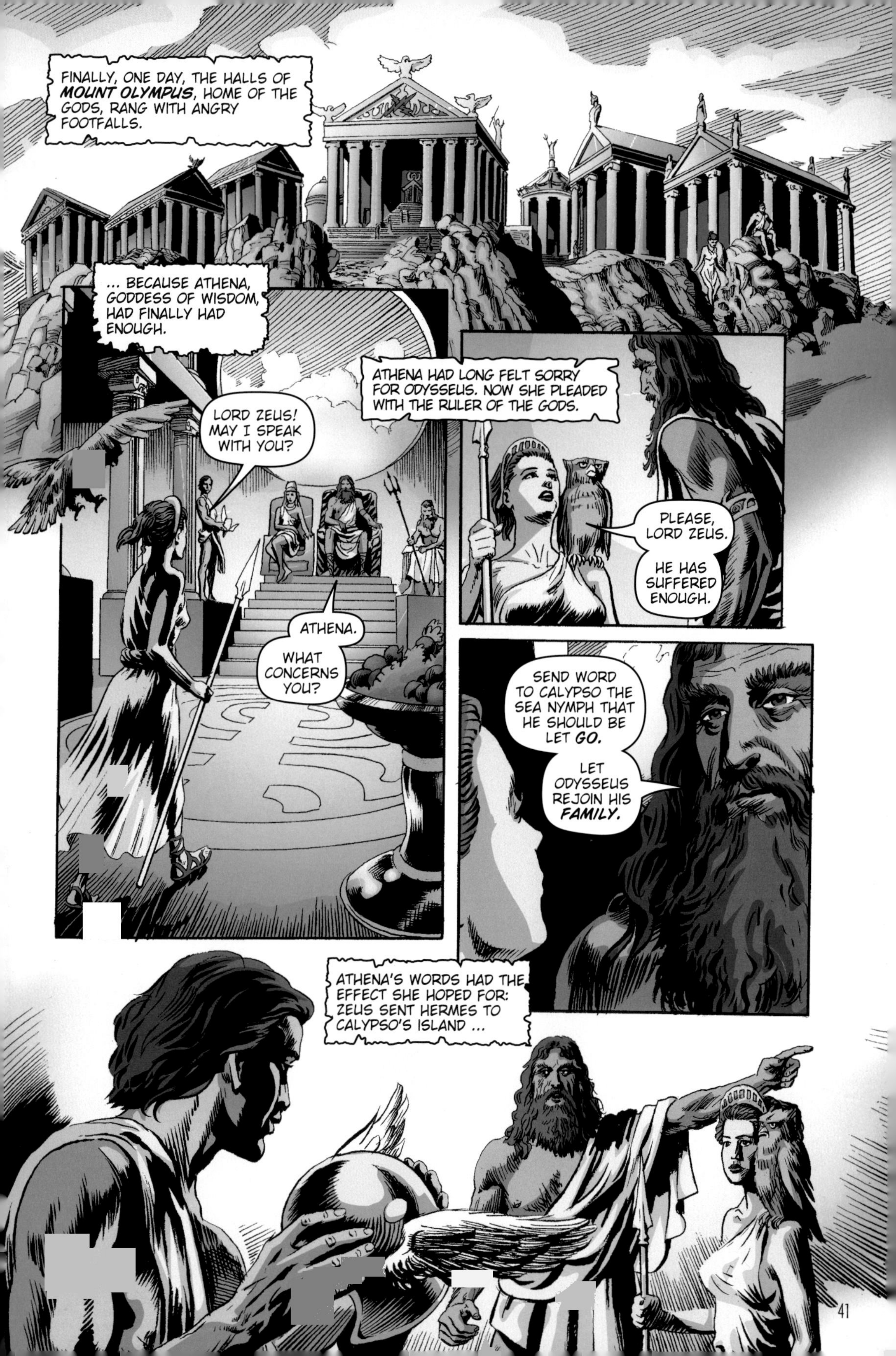
FINALLY, ONE DAY, THE HALLS OF MOUNT OLYMPUS, HOME OF THE GODS, RANG WITH ANGRY FOOTFALLS.
... BECAUSE ATHENA, GODDESS OF WISDOM, HAD FINALLY HAD ENOUGH.
LORD ZEUS! MAY I SPEAK WITH YOU?
ATHENA.
WHAT CONCERNS YOU?
ATHENA HAD LONG FELT SORRY FOR ODYSSEUS. NOW SHE PLEADED WITH THE RULER OF THE GODS.
PLEASE, LORD ZEUS.
HE HAS SUFFERED ENOUGH.
SEND WORD TO CALYPSO THE SEA NYMPH THAT HE SHOULD BE LET GO.
LET ODYSSEUS REJOIN HIS FAMILY.
ATHENA'S WORDS HAD THE EFFECT SHE HOPED FOR: ZEUS SENT HERMES TO CALYPSO'S ISLAND ...

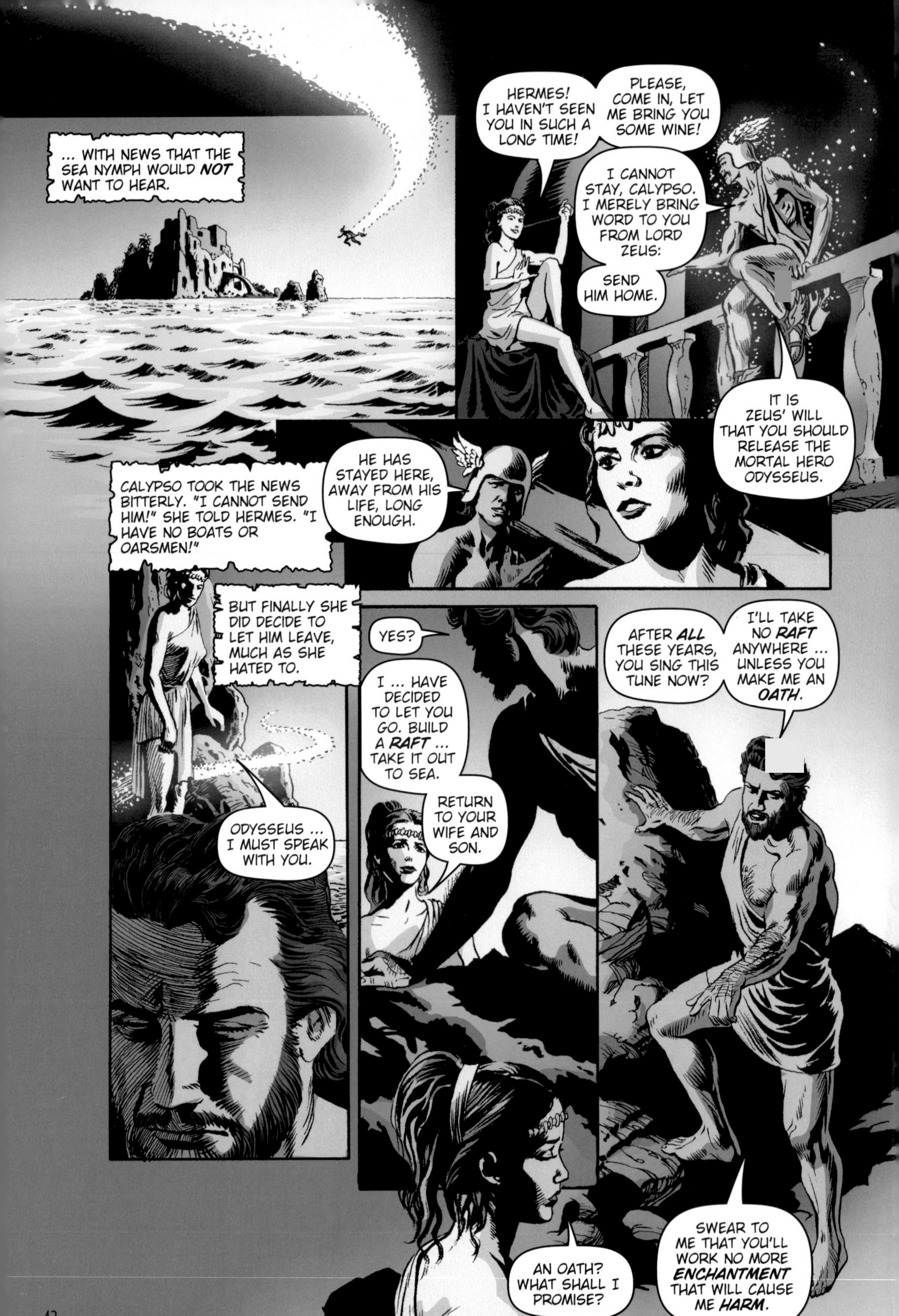
... WITH NEWS THAT THE SEA NYMPH WOULD NOT WANT TO HEAR.
HERMES! I HAVEN'T SEEN YOU IN SUCH A LONG TIME!
PLEASE, COME IN, LET ME BRING YOU SOME WINE!
I CANNOT STAY, CALYPSO. I MERELY BRING WORD TO YOU FROM LORD ZEUS:
SEND HIM HOME.
IT IS ZEUS' WILL THAT YOU SHOULD RELEASE THE MORTAL HERO ODYSSEUS.
CALYPSO TOOK THE NEWS BITTERLY. "I CANNOT SEND HIM!" SHE TOLD HERMES. "I HAVE NO BOATS OR OARSMEN!"
HE HAS STAYED HERE, AWAY FROM HIS LIFE, LONG ENOUGH.
BUT FINALLY SHE DID DECIDE TO LET HIM LEAVE, MUCH AS SHE HATED TO.
ODYSSEUS ... I MUST SPEAK WITH YOU.
YES?
I ... HAVE DECIDED TO LET YOU GO. BUILD A RAFT ... TAKE IT OUT TO SEA.
RETURN TO YOUR WIFE AND SON.
AFTER ALL THESE YEARS, YOU SING THIS TUNE NOW?
I'LL TAKE NO RAFT ANYWHERE ... UNLESS YOU MAKE ME AN OATH.
AN OATH? WHAT SHALL I PROMISE?
SWEAR TO ME THAT YOU'LL WORK NO MORE ENCHANTMENT THAT WILL CAUSE ME HARM.

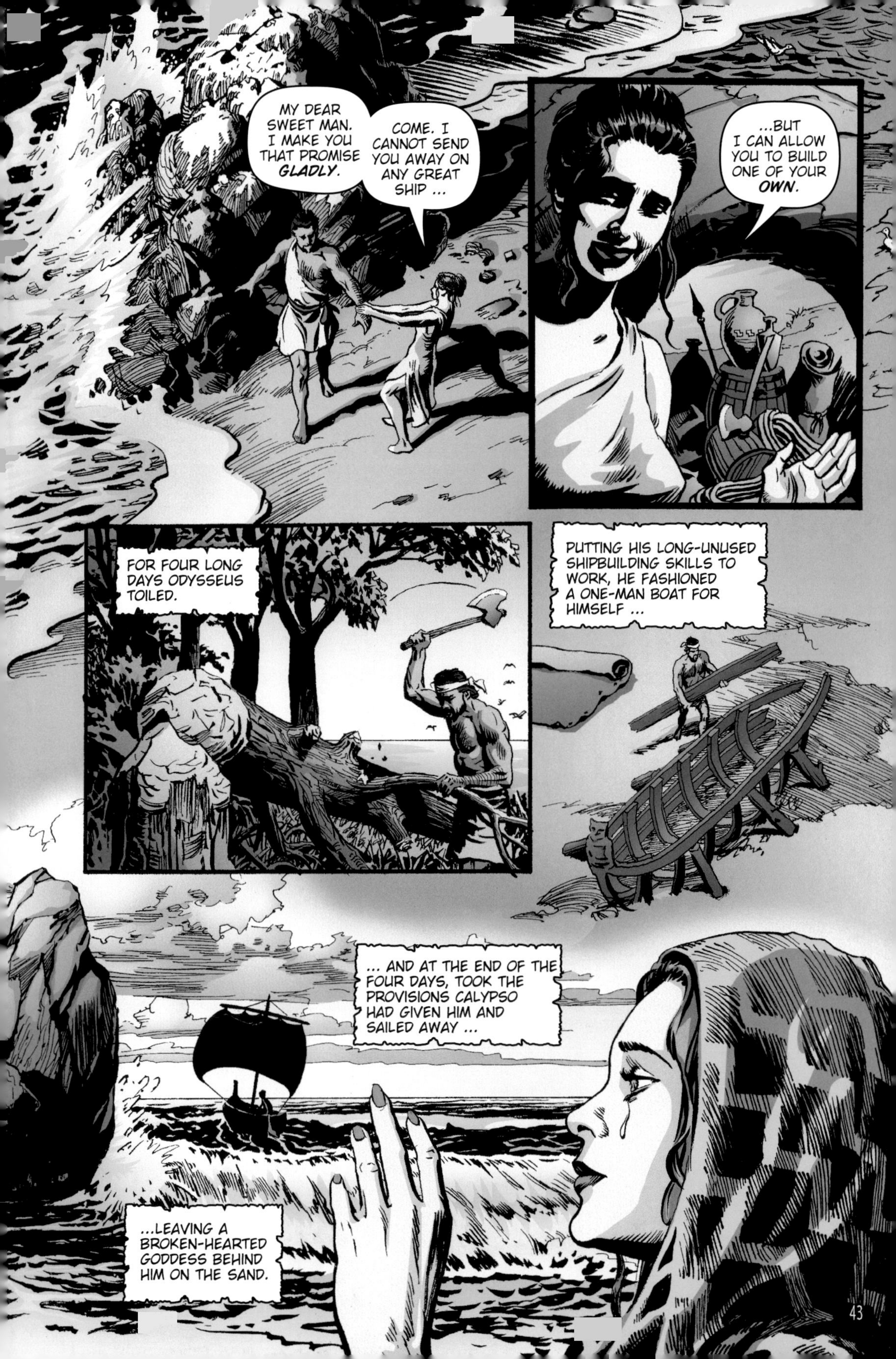

MY DEAR SWEET MAN. I MAKE YOU THAT PROMISE GLADLY.
COME. I CANNOT SEND YOU AWAY ON ANY GREAT SHIP ...
...BUT I CAN ALLOW YOU TO BUILD ONE OF YOUR OWN.
FOR FOUR LONG DAYS ODYSSEUS TOILED.
PUTTING HIS LONG-UNUSED SHIPBUILDING SKILLS TO WORK, HE FASHIONED A ONE-MAN BOAT FOR HIMSELF ...
... AND AT THE END OF THE FOUR DAYS, TOOK THE PROVISIONS CALYPSO HAD GIVEN HIM AND SAILED AWAY ...
...LEAVING A BROKEN-HEARTED GODDESS BEHIND HIM ON THE SAND.

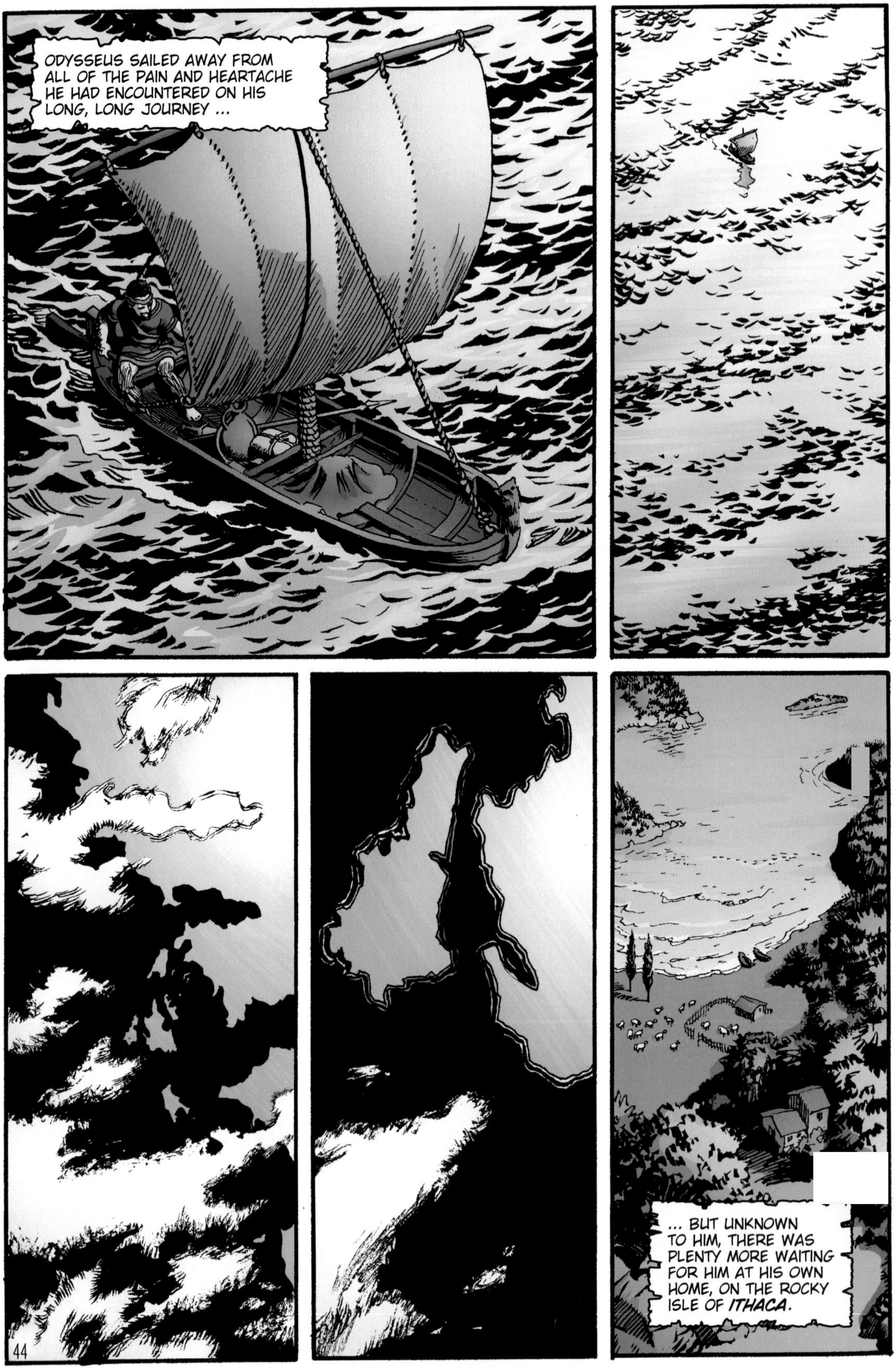
ODYSSEUS SAILED AWAY FROM ALL OF THE PAIN AND HEARTACHE HE HAD ENCOUNTERED ON HIS LONG, LONG JOURNEY ...
... BUT UNKNOWN TO HIM, THERE WAS PLENTY MORE WAITING FOR HIM AT HIS OWN HOME, ON THE ROCKY ISLE OF *ITHACA*.

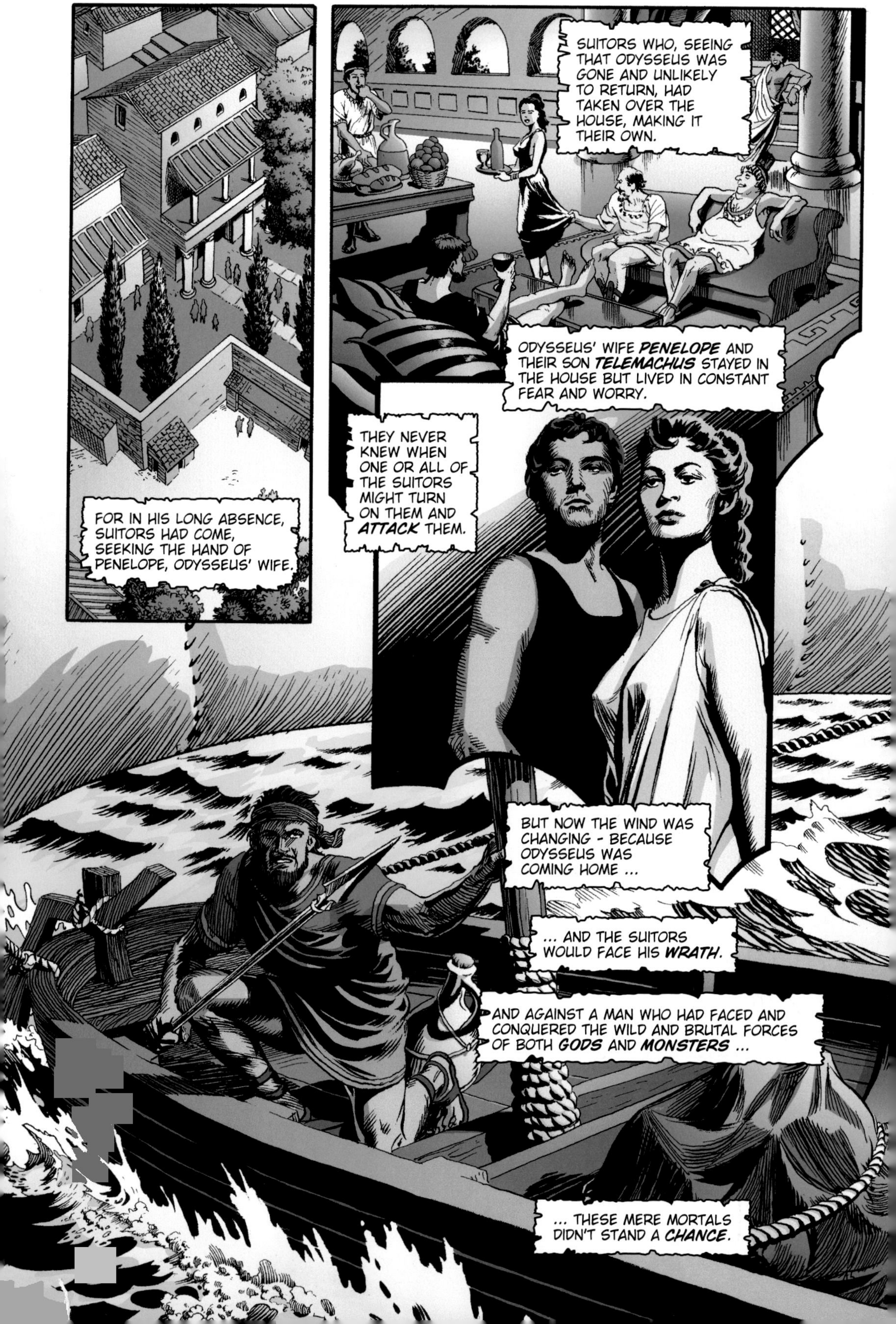
FOR IN HIS LONG ABSENCE, SUITORS HAD COME, SEEKING THE HAND OF PENELOPE, ODYSSEUS' WIFE.
SUITORS WHO, SEEING THAT ODYSSEUS WAS GONE AND UNLIKELY TO RETURN, HAD TAKEN OVER THE HOUSE, MAKING IT THEIR OWN.
ODYSSEUS' WIFE PENELOPE AND THEIR SON TELEMACHUS STAYED IN THE HOUSE BUT LIVED IN CONSTANT FEAR AND WORRY.
THEY NEVER KNEW WHEN ONE OR ALL OF THE SUITORS MIGHT TURN ON THEM AND ATTACK THEM.
BUT NOW THE WIND WAS CHANGING - BECAUSE ODYSSEUS WAS COMING HOME ...
... AND THE SUITORS WOULD FACE HIS WRATH.
AND AGAINST A MAN WHO HAD FACED AND CONQUERED THE WILD AND BRUTAL FORCES OF BOTH GODS AND MONSTERS ...
... THESE MERE MORTALS DIDN'T STAND A CHANCE.

GLOSSARY AND PRONUNCIATION GUIDE

ATHENA (uh-*thee*-nuh): the Greek goddess of wisdom

CHARYBDIS (kuh-*rib*-duhs): a violent whirlpool that sucks up ships, destroys them, and spits them out

CIRCE (*sur*-see): a witch whom Odysseus and his men encounter on their journey home to Ithaca

CYCLOPS (*sy*-klops): one of a race of mythical giants with a single eye in the middle of their foreheads. The plural form is Cylopes.

DESERT: to flee or abandon one's duties without permission

EURYLOCHUS (yur-*ril*-eh-kus): Odysseus' trusted second-in-command

HELIOS (*hee*-lee-us): the Greek god of the sun

HEPHAISTOS (heh-*fes*-tus): the blacksmith god

HERMES (*hur*-meez): the messenger of the gods on Mount Olympus

ITHACA: Odysseus' homeland; a Greek island

LAISTRYGONIANS (ly-struh-*go*-nee-uns): a race of fierce giants that Odysseus and his men encounter on their journey home to Ithaca

ODYSSEUS (oh-*dis*-see-uhs): king of Ithaca

PENELOPE (peh-*nel*-oh-pee): wife of Odysseus

POLYPHEMUS (pahl-ee-*fee*-muhs): the fearsome Cyclops whom Odysseus and his men encounter on their journey home to Ithaca

POSEIDON (poh-*sy*-duhn): the Greek god of the sea

PROVISIONS: a stock of supplies, such as food and water

SCYLLA (*si*-luh): a six-headed monster that can devour six sailors in one stroke

STRAIT: a narrow passageway connecting two large bodies of water

SUITORS: one who courts a woman or seeks to marry her

TALISMAN: an object that is believed to defend against evil or bring good fortune

TELEMACHUS (tel-*lem*-ah-kus): Odysseus' son

TROJAN WAR: a brutal ten-year war fought between the Trojans and the Greeks around 1200 B.C.

ZEUS (*zoos*): king of the Greek gods

FURTHER READING, WEBSITES, AND MOVIES

Bolton, Lesley. *The Everything Classical Mythology Book: Greek and Roman Gods, Goddesses, Heroes, and Monsters from Ares to Zeus.* Avon, MA: Adams Media Corporation, 2002. This who's who guide introduces young readers to Greek and Roman mythology.

Day, Nancy. *Your Travel Guide to Ancient Greece.* Minneapolis: Twenty-First Century Books, 2001. Day prepares readers for a trip back to ancient Greece, including which cities to visit, how to get around, what to wear, and how to fit in with the locals.

Fontes, Ron, and Justine Fontes. *The Trojan Horse: The Fall of Troy.* Minneapolis: Graphic Universe, 2007. Learn more about the Trojan War, the exciting story that precedes the *Odyssey.*

MythWeb. http://www.mythweb.com/index.html. This site, with a searchable encyclopedia, provides readers with information on gods, goddesses, and places in Greek myth, as well as ample information about Homer's *Odyssey.*

The Odyssey. DVD. Directed by Andrei Konchalovsky. Vancouver, British Columbia, Canada: Lions Gate Entertainment, 1997. This made-for-TV movie stars Armand Assante as Odysseus and uses excellent special effects to portray the thrilling tale of Odysseus' adventures.

CREATING *ODYSSEUS: ESCAPING POSEIDON'S CURSE*

To retell this ancient story for modern readers, Dan Jolley consulted several translations of the *Odyssey,* both prose and verse versions. Artist Thomas Yeates used historical and traditional sources to shape the story's visual details—from images on ancient Greek vases to sculpture and other artwork. David Mulroy of the University of Wisconsin-Milwaukee ensured the accuracy of the story's historical and visual details. Together, the text and the art bring to life this story from ancient Greece.

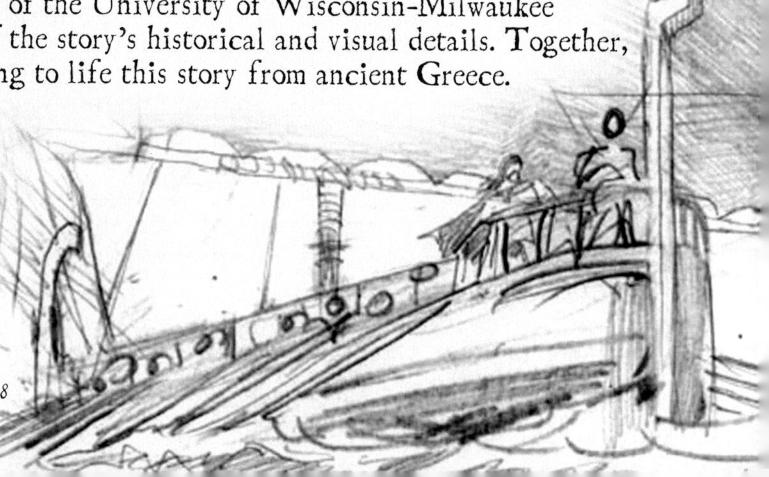

original pencil from page 28

INDEX

Aiaia, 21, 27
Athena, 7, 8, 24, 41

Calypso, 39–43
Charybdis, 28, 33, 37
Circe, 22–29, 32, 34, 40
Cyclopes, land of, 13

Eurylochus, 9, 12, 21–24, 27, 29, 31, 35

Helios' cattle, 34–36
Hermes, 24, 26, 41, 42

Laistrygonians, 21
lotus eaters, 9–11

Penelope, 7, 45
Polyphemus (cyclops), 15–21
Poseidon, 8, 19, 20

Scylla, 28, 32, 33
sirens, 28–31

Telemachus, 7, 45
Trojan Horse, 7
Trojan War, 6, 7

Zeus, 8, 10, 15, 16, 36, 41, 42

ABOUT THE AUTHOR AND THE ARTIST

DAN JOLLEY began his writing career in the early 1990s. His limited series *Obergeist* was voted Best Horror Comic of 2001 by *Wizard Magazine*, and his DC Comics project *JSA: The Unholy Three* received an Eisner Award nomination (the comics industry's highest honor) for Best Limited Series of 2003. In recent years, he has co-written two novels based on licensed properties: *Star Trek SCE: Some Assembly Required*, and *Vengeance*, from the television series *Angel*. May of 2007 will see the debut of Dan's first solo novel series, an original Young Adult sci-fi espionage story called *Alex, Unlimited*, published by a joint venture of TokyoPop and HarperCollins. Dan lives in Cary, North Carolina, where he spends way too much time playing video games.

THOMAS YEATES began his art training in high school and continued at Utah State University and Sacramento State University. Subsequently, he was a member of the first class at Joe Kubert's School, a trade program for aspiring comic book artists in New Jersey. Yeates has worked as an illustrator for DC Comics, Marvel, Dark Horse, and many other companies, drawing Tarzan, Zorro, the Swamp Thing, Time Spirits, Captain America, and Conan. For the Graphic Myths and Legends series, he illustrated *King Arthur: Excalibur Unsheathed*, *Robin Hood: Outlaw of Sherwood Forest*, and *Atalanta: The Race against Destiny*. Yeates lives in northern California with his wife and daughter.